MENTAL HEALTH MATTERS

UNDERSTANDING EATING DISORDERS

DONNA REYNOLDS

ROSEN PUBLISHING

Published in 2026 by The Rosen Publishing Group, Inc.
2544 Clinton Street, Buffalo, NY 14224

Portions of this work were originally authored by Elizabeth Silverthorne and published as *Anorexia and Bulimia*. All new material this edition authored by Donna Reynolds.

Cataloging-in-Publication Data

Names: Reynolds, Donna, 1976-.
Title: Understanding eating disorders / Donna Reynolds.
Description: First edition. | Buffalo, NY : Rosen Publishing, 2026. | Series: Mental health matters | Includes glossary and index.
Identifiers: ISBN 9781499479638 (pbk.) | ISBN 9781499479645 (library bound) | ISBN 9781499479652 (ebook)
Subjects: LCSH: Eating disorders--Juvenile literature. | Eating disorders--Treatment--Juvenile literature.
Classification: LCC RC552.E18 R49 2026 | DDC 616.85'26 --dc23

Manufactured in the United States of America

CPSIA Compliance Information: Batch #CSRYA26. For further information, contact Rosen Publishing at 1-800-237-9932.

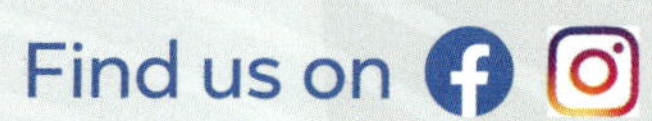

CONTENTS

FOREWORD

There are many misconceptions about illness, especially mental illness. Advances in scientific knowledge have increased our understanding of many diseases and disorders, including the common cold, diabetes, and cancer. Many of these sicknesses and chronic conditions cause physical symptoms that people can see and understand, and their causes are often easy to explain.

The same cannot always be said for mental illnesses. Mental disorders are just as common as physical disorders, but without physical symptoms, they are often dismissed. People tend to believe that a mental illness is easy to get over with enough willpower. They may call people with mental illnesses names such as "lazy" and "attention-seeking." Some people even deny that mental illnesses exist at all.

People who have been convinced by those around them that they have a problem of willpower rather than a treatable illness often go undiagnosed for years. This can cause a lot of suffering; people with an undiagnosed mental disorder often understand that they are experiencing the world in a different way than their peers, but they have no one to turn to for answers. Many feel guilty about not being able to control their symptoms, not realizing that this is as impractical as telling someone with a broken leg that they should be able to walk without pain if they simply try hard enough.

In recent years, the stigma, or perceived shame, of mental illness has decreased. More people, especially young people, are willing to seek therapy and talk openly about their diagnosed mental illnesses. However, this has also led to a rise in misinformation, which can be spread through personal anecdotes, social media, and even news sources. The misuse of "therapy speak" and armchair diagnoses by internet commenters are two growing problems. Furthermore, although the stigma has lessened, it has not disappeared completely. People sometimes use mental illnesses as insults. Someone who displays normal ranges of emotion, for example, may be called "bipolar" as an insult. This shows a lack of understanding about bipolar disorder and furthers the stigma around this disorder by making it sound like a negative aspect of who a person is.

This series aims to offer accurate information about mental illnesses so young adults will have a better understanding of them. Each volume discusses the symptoms of a particular illness, ways it is currently being treated, and the research that is being done to understand it further. Advice for people who may be suffering from a disorder is included, as well as information for their loved ones about how best to support them.

With fully cited quotes, a list of recommended books and websites for further research, and informational charts, this series provides young adults with a factual introduction to common mental illnesses. By learning more about these disorders, they will be better able to show compassion to people who are dealing with mental illnesses and take charge of their own mental health.

MENTAL AND PHYSICAL

Eating is something all people have to do to stay alive. It gives the body fuel to run properly and energy to take a walk, concentrate on a book, or do activities with family and friends. Food can also be a source of joy, a way to connect with loved ones, and a link to a person's culture. However, instead of seeing food in these beneficial ways, many people spend a lot of time preoccupied with what and how much they are eating. They are influenced by what their friends are eating, celebrity diets, and what they hear on talk shows.

With so many people following different diets—such as paleo, keto, and intermittent fasting—it can be hard to spot disordered eating. However, many of these diets have strict rules that promote restricting or cutting out certain foods, which can cause a person long-term psychological harm and can lead to physical problems. For many, the line between following these diets and developing an eating disorder is troublingly blurry. Over time, what can simply be called disordered eating—only eating at certain times of day, in specific quantities, or a few categories of food, for example—can worsen into a clinically diagnosable eating disorder. About 9 percent of the U.S. population will have an eating disorder at some point in their life.

Binge eating disorder (BED), anorexia nervosa, and bulimia nervosa are three major categories of these disorders. BED is the most common eating disorder in the United States; it affects three times as many people as anorexia and bulimia combined. It is characterized by eating large amounts of food in a short period of time, even if the person eating is not actually hungry. Anorexia is characterized by behaviors that allow a person to eat as little as possible to achieve a low body weight. Behaviors of bulimia include eating large amounts of food followed by some kind of purging, either by abuse of laxatives (drugs that make a person have to go to the bathroom), excessive exercise, or vomiting. Less common eating disorders include avoidant/restrictive food intake disorder (ARFID), where people reject many foods because they do not like the texture or have anxiety about eating, and pica, where people have cravings for non-food items such as dirt, chalk, or clay.

Eating is meant to be an enjoyable experience. However, for almost 30 million Americans, it is a source of distress that is so extreme and debilitating it interferes with basic functions and can even be life-threatening.

A NEW FOCUS

Eating disorders are not a creation of the 20th and 21st centuries, but it was not until around the 1980s that they were recognized in the United States as a serious problem.

In 1979, Aimee Liu published *Solitaire*, a memoir about her struggles with an eating disorder that began when she was a teenager. (She does not call herself a sufferer of anorexia because when she wrote the book at age 25, she did not know the name for her persistent eating issues.) The book was groundbreaking. It was one of the first narratives of this kind, telling the story of a teenage girl trying to lose weight and the harmful obsession it became.

Then, in 1983, the world was shocked by the death of Karen Carpenter, the drummer and lead singer of the famous musical duo The Carpenters. She was only 32 years old at the time of her death and had been suffering from anorexia since her teen years, after someone had told her she was chubby. Carpenter was the first celebrity to die of an eating disorder in the public eye. Her death encouraged more celebrities to come forward with their own troubling stories.

Even knowing that other people were experiencing the same thing, it was still difficult for some to admit. After 17 years of dealing with bulimia, singer and dancer Paula Abdul—who later went on to be a judge on *American Idol*—spoke out about her eating disorder in 1995. Like many, her struggles began when she was growing up. Then, as a professional dancer, the 5-foot 2-inch (1.5 m) tall Abdul felt pressure to compete with other taller, thinner dancers. She has continued to raise awareness about

Karen Carpenter's death brought the danger of eating disorders to the world's attention.

eating disorders since opening up about her struggles.

Celebrities continue to share stories of their struggles with eating disorders today. Lady Gaga, Kesha, Taylor Swift, Ed Sheeran, and Demi Lovato are some examples of famous people who have spoken about their experiences.

Demi Lovato has spoken openly about her mental health.

SUFFERING SILENTLY

While stories of celebrities shine a spotlight on eating disorders and recovery, these brave, outspoken men and women are a very small percentage of those who deal with eating disorders every day. Most suffer quietly, just trying to get through their school day or workday without anyone noticing their disordered behaviors.

Understanding why a friend or family member might be turning to these behaviors can be difficult. It can seem like they are choosing to do themselves harm and that they could stop if they wanted to.

However, it is important to know that the causes of eating disorders are varied, from family history to issues with anxiety and depression. Treatment for these illnesses can be lifelong, but with supportive, caring people around them, eating disorder sufferers have a greater chance of recovery. By learning the signs of eating disorders, anyone could be the catalyst for someone realizing they need help and seeking it out.

Eating disorders are more than just a mental health problem; they can cause serious physical problems and may lead to death. In fact, the mortality, or death, rates for eating disorders are some of the highest of any mental health disorder, with anorexia being the highest. From celebrity spokespeople to concerned friends, anyone who raises awareness about these conditions could save lives—even if it is just a comment about enjoying lunch instead of focusing on its calorie content.

CHAPTER ONE

WHAT ARE EATING DISORDERS?

In the past, many people believed that only wealthy young women, especially white women, were affected by eating disorders. However, according to the National Eating Disorders Association (NEDA), eating disorders are "serious but treatable mental and physical illnesses that can affect people of every age, sex, gender, race, ethnicity, and socioeconomic group."[1] That means anyone can develop an eating disorder no matter who they are or what their family is like.

Since scientists and doctors do not know exactly what causes someone to develop an eating disorder, more research is being done every year to try to figure it out. Today, the reasons behind why some people develop an eating disorder and the medical community's view of these disorders are very different than they were in the past. This has also changed the public's view of those with eating disorders.

A BRIEF HISTORY

Eating disorders as they are diagnosed and described today are modern disorders. However, the behaviors common to eating disorders have been recorded since ancient times. Self-starvation practices have been traced to religious beliefs during the Middle Ages. Hermits of the Christian faith would refuse to eat in an attempt to achieve spiritual purity, and Saint Jerome preached the benefits of this lifestyle choice. However, most of the time, records of food restriction and self-starvation have been linked to women. These women were frequently trying to become closer to God by denying themselves food, but this often led to death. Saint Catherine of Siena was one such casualty. She lived from 1347 to 1380 CE and was well known for eating very little for long periods of time. She and others believed they could prove how devoted they were to God by doing

Miss A—, No. 1.

Miss A—, No. 2.

These pictures are from a scientific paper on anorexia from the 1800s. The top picture shows "MIss A" with anorexia in 1866.The bottom shows her after recovery in 1870.

so, or they may have believed that their desire for food was sinful because they should not desire material things.

During the Renaissance, the reasons for self-starvation behaviors began to shift away from the religious. Material reasons began to become part of the equation as beauty ideals shifted. In the past, a heavier body type was considered beautiful, but over time, slimness became the ideal. By the late 1770s, medical and psychological reasons for what we now know as disordered eating began to be discussed, though it was still described by some as possibly being caused by an "ill and morbid state of the spirits."[2]

By the 1800s, medical professionals were observing and writing about a variety of cases of self-starvation and other disordered eating behaviors. The first medical paper that tried to describe these behaviors came out in 1860. Not long after, Sir William Gull called collections of behaviors like this "anorexia nervosa." Previously, a person who showed such behavior might be considered to have "hysteria," but Gull saw a separate disorder. He said it could happen in both men and women. His work and that of others made it clear they considered the disorder psychological. The late 1880s brought more descriptions of disordered eating behaviors. By the early 1900s, behaviors that are now associated with bulimia nervosa were also being noted.

THE 20TH AND 21ST CENTURIES

In 1952, the American Psychological Association (APA) released the first *Diagnostic and Statistical Manual* (*DSM-I*), a listing of all recognized mental health disorders that included diagnostic criteria and descriptions. This manual included one

A NEWER DISORDER

Although anorexia and bulimia have been documented for centuries, binge eating disorder seems to be fairly new. This may have something to do with increased access to food in modern times, although without documentation, there is no way to know for sure. It was first described in 1959 by a psychiatrist called Albert Stunkard, who called it "night eating syndrome." Later, after he realized binges could happen at any time of day, the name was changed to binge eating disorder.

Night eating syndrome (NES) is still a type of eating disorder, but with different symptoms than BED. With BED, a person feels an uncontrollable urge to eat even when they are not hungry and long past the time when they start feeling uncomfortably full. It is different than bulimia because the person does not take any actions to "undo" their binge, such as vomiting or over-exercising. With NES, a person wakes up multiple times during the night and feels as though they must eat something in order to be able to fall back asleep.

eating disorder: anorexia nervosa. In 1968, the second edition (*DSM-II*) moved the disorder to a grouping called special symptoms/feeding disturbances. This grouping also included pica and rumination, a disorder characterized by a person regurgitating food to chew it again.

The 1970s proved to be a turning point in the history of eating disorders. At this time, medical professionals were seeing a rise in both anorexia and the behaviors associated with bulimia, as well as a rise in obesity. Important books and articles about eating disorders were published, including Dr. Hilde Bruch's *Eating Disorders: Obesity, Anorexia Nervosa, and the Person Within*. The first major paper discussing cases of bulimia came out too. Gerard Russell, a British psychologist, had begun noting differences between anorexia and another distinct eating disorder in 1972, when he met a woman who came to him for

The *DSM* is updated periodically as research uncovers new information.

anorexia treatment but did not present with the signs of anorexia. After several years of observing other similar cases, he published "Bulimia Nervosa: An Ominous Variant of Anorexia Nervosa" in 1979, including the differences between patients with anorexia and the now-named bulimia.

When the *DSM-III* came out in 1980, a section focusing solely on eating disorders was added. This edition of the *DSM*, which arrived in 1987, included bulimia as its own category under the heading of eating disorders. By then, the death of Karen Carpenter and other public discussions of eating disorders had brought these disorders into the spotlight in the media and in the psychiatric community.

Since then, the diagnostic criteria have only become more refined with each edition and revision of the *DSM* as medical professionals learn more about why some people develop eating disorders, the signs of these disorders, and proper treatments.

BED, ARFID, anorexia, bulimia, rumination disorder, and pica each have their own listing in the fifth edition of the *DSM*. Other categories include other specified feeding and eating disorders (OSFED), for eating disorders that do not fall neatly into one of those four categories, and unspecified feeding or eating disorder (UFED), for disordered eating that affects a person's life but does not meet the criteria for any of the other listed eating disorders.

A CLOSER LOOK AT ANOREXIA

Someone who suffers from anorexia worries a lot about how their body looks and manages their food intake with that in mind. They typically try to lose weight or maintain a very low body weight by severely limiting the amount of food they eat. They may skip meals and lie about having eaten. When they eat with others, they may move food around on their plate without eating it, or they may hide some of it in their napkin. They may take a very long time to eat very little. For example, one person with anorexia described taking an hour to eat her meal, which consisted only of one apple. Another told how she divided a cookie into 32 sections to eat over several days. Another way people with anorexia attempt to control the size of their body is through excessive, compulsive exercise. The size of their body becomes the most important part of their self-esteem.

Anorexia is the medical term for "loss of appetite," and sometimes a medical chart will list anorexia for a person who has lost their appetite

People who have an eating disorder may push their food around on their plate without actually eating any of it.

due to pain or nausea. Anorexia nervosa is often shortened simply to anorexia, but it is not simply a loss of appetite. In fact, when many people with anorexia first begin to restrict their food, they may be very hungry. Instead of fulfilling their needs, they ignore them by refusing to eat. Over time, as their body gets used to a smaller amount of food, they may feel less hungry—but this does not mean they do not need to eat. It just means their body has stopped sending them signals about it as often.

A CLOSER LOOK AT BED

The word "binge" is often used to describe excess drinking or consuming a large amount of something, such as a TV show, in a short amount of time. Sometimes, people who occasionally eat more than normal might say they "binged" on ice cream or potato chips. When eating disorder experts use the term "binge," they are generally referring to eating a large amount of food in combination with a feeling of loss of control or dissociation, which is a feeling of being disconnected from a person's own thoughts or actions.

Christopher G. Fairburn, a specialist in treating binge eating disorder, described the aftermath of a binge:

> *Those who binge may say they experience some immediate, though temporary positive feelings. For example, they may feel a sense of relief. Feelings of hunger and deprivation will have disappeared, and perhaps the depression or anxiety that may have triggered the binge has been displaced. But these positive effects are soon replaced by feelings of shame, disgust, and guilt.*[1]

Like anorexia and bulimia, BED is dangerous. People who binge characteristically eat large quantities of food in short periods of time, eat when not hungry, eat in secret, and feel distress and guilt over their behavior despite feeling unable to control it. For a long time, it was known as compulsive overeating. In early editions of the *DSM*, binge eating was mentioned as a sign of bulimia. In 2013, BED was listed as a separate category from bulimia in the *DSM-5*.

Not all binge eaters are overweight. However, body size is not necessarily an accurate indicator of health, and BED can cause life-threatening health problems no matter who is experiencing it. According to the Eating Recovery Center, risks associated with BED include:

- *High blood pressure*
- *High cholesterol*
- *Heart disease*
- *Type II diabetes mellitus*[2]

1. Christopher G. Fairburn, *Overcoming Binge Eating*. New York, NY: Guilford, 1995, p. 20.

2. "Binge Eating Disorder (BED) Health Risks," Eating Recovery Center, accessed on September 28, 2018. www.eatingrecoverycenter.com/conditions/binge-eating/health-risks.

The *DSM* includes two types of anorexia: restricting and binge eating/purging. Those who are considered restricting type keep the calories they take in very low by restricting their food and may exercise excessively. Someone with the binge eating/purge type of anorexia also restricts food taken in but also may self-induce vomiting or use laxatives, diuretics, or enemas to cause them to go to the bathroom more frequently than normal so they can get the food they eat out of their system before their body can absorb it. This prevents them from absorbing essential nutrients. Although the symptoms of this type of anorexia are similar to the symptoms of bulimia, someone with binge eating/purge type anorexia loses much more weight than someone with bulimia. This extreme weight loss is an important diagnostic criterion.

A CLOSER LOOK AT BULIMIA

The signs of bulimia are often not as apparent as those of anorexia. Similar to anorexia, a person with bulimia gets their sense of self-worth from what they and others think of their body's shape or size.

Those with bulimia eat very large food portions. This might be a whole cake instead of a slice, or a box of cookies instead of just a few. Then, filled with horror at the idea of gaining weight, they engage in vomiting or misuse laxatives, diuretics, or enemas to purge the food from their bodies. They may also excessively exercise, fast, or misuse medication. Because their behavior takes place in secret and their appearance typically changes less than that of someone with anorexia, sufferers of bulimia are sometimes able to hide their disease for years.

COMMON AND DEADLY

The National Institute of Mental Health (NIMH) lists anorexia and bulimia as the two deadliest eating disorders. BED, while more common and still dangerous, tends to kill fewer people. Eating disorder sufferers often try to hide their disorder, and many do not seek out an official diagnosis or treatment out of fear of gaining weight in recovery. This behavior makes it impossible to know exactly how many people are suffering from eating disorders, at what age they first developed symptoms, or how they are being affected by them. Data from reliable sources, however, shows that despite growing awareness of the seriousness of these diseases, the number of people with them is increasing. In fact, experts agree that eating disorders have reached epidemic levels in America, and many segments of the population are at risk.

According to the Cleveland Clinic, both anorexia and bulimia most often begin occurring in adolescence. However, children under age 12 can also suffer from these eating disorders. The number of sufferers in this age group has been on the rise since the 1990s and includes both boys and girls. Since the COVID-19 pandemic, experts have noticed a troubling trend: Eating disorders are beginning at a younger age.

Additionally, compared to past generations, these young patients are "sicker than they were before, and they're more complicated than they were before,"[3] according to Melissa Freizinger, the associate director of the eating disorder program at Boston Children's Hospital in Massachusetts. More people are being admitted to hospitals with severe mental and physical health problems, which experts say were likely either caused or made worse by the fear, isolation, and uncertainty of the pandemic. Social media also plays a very large role, as young people see an idealized—and often fake—idea of what a body "should" look like to be considered beautiful.

The places with the highest numbers of eating disorders are the United States, Europe, Canada, South Africa, and New Zealand. All of these are industrialized societies that have more than enough food and idealize thinness. Some ethnic groups in the United States are more likely to develop eating disorders, such as Latina, Native American, and Black women. None of these groups on their own has as high a number of people with eating disorders as the white population, but people of color in general are at high risk of developing eating disorders. The NEDA reported that Black teens have a 50 percent greater chance of bingeing and

Certain factors can point to an increased risk for developing an eating disorder. However, there is no way to tell for certain who will develop an eating disorder. People of all races and genders are affected.

ORTHOREXIA

Some people have eating disorders that are not widely shared within the general population. These tend to fall under the category of unspecified feeding or eating disorders (UFED). One example is orthorexia. This is an obsession with "healthy" eating that is taken to such an extreme that it becomes unhealthy.

Orthorexia can be difficult to recognize because the benefits of eating "healthy" foods are discussed frequently. However, this disorder is different than just eating nutritious foods. Some symptoms include refusing to eat any food that the person does not consider healthy; cutting out carbs, fats, or other necessary food groups in the mistaken belief that all the foods in those categories are unhealthy; feeling and acting superior about their food choices and telling other people what they should or should not eat; showing distress when foods they consider "healthy enough" are not available; and obsessing over the ingredients in everything they eat.

purging than white teens. A study has also shown that those who are Latine have also been found to be more likely to suffer from bulimia than non-Latine adolescents. Socioeconomic status may also play a role in who develops eating disorders. The NEDA reported that teen girls from low-income families are 153 percent more likely to develop an eating disorder. People who are nonbinary or transgender are also much more likely to suffer from an eating disorder than people who are cisgender. All of this data debunks the common belief that anorexia and bulimia are found most often in upper class, white, cis teenage women.

Additionally, though more women overall suffer from eating disorders, a significant number of men deal with anorexia, bulimia, BED, and other eating disorders. In the United States, about one-third of the 30 million people who develop an eating disorder in their lifetime are men. According to the National Eating Disorders Collaboration

Eating a variety of nutritious foods is an important part of taking care of the body. However, people can become so obsessed with the idea of health that it becomes an eating disorder.

(NEDC), men represent about 20 percent of anorexia patients, 30 percent of those with bulimia, 43 percent of those with BED, and 67 percent of people with ARFID. Former professional baseball player Mike Marjama retired from the Seattle Mariners in 2018 to work with the NEDA. He believes more attention needs to be focused on the large number of men who suffer from eating disorders. Marjama said, "There are men who have told me they've suffered with this illness for 30 or 40 years and felt like they haven't been able to say anything about it."[4] Singer Ed Sheeran has also opened up about his struggle with BED. He noted that it was difficult for him to feel like he could come forward because of the stereotype that eating disorders are not "manly."

Ed Sheeran has spoken up not only about his eating disorder, but about the extra stigma men face when they have one.

Regardless of a sufferer's age, sex, gender, sexual orientation, or ethnic background, eating disorders are serious illnesses and should be treated as such. They often present in certain ways that may tip off family members, friends, and doctors to a person's disordered eating behaviors. Understanding these signs and symptoms can save a life.

SYMPTOMS

Eating disorders often start slowly. Few people with anorexia, for example, jump straight to not eating anything. They may start by eating less, counting calories obsessively, and restricting certain types of foods. As time goes on, these disordered behaviors worsen and become full-blown anorexia.

The gradual pace of eating disorders allows them to develop quietly because many who suffer from eating disorders deny that anything is wrong. Their actions often take place in secret. Additionally, because exercising and dieting are so accepted in American culture and normalized on social media, it may take family and friends a long time to notice that someone has crossed the line into an eating disorder.

However, there are many signs of eating disorders that can be recognized. These are often used in diagnosis—the formal, medical acknowledgement that someone is experiencing a problem that needs treatment.

SYMPTOMS OF ANOREXIA

At first, it might not be obvious that someone is suffering from anorexia. They may say they are not hungry or ate earlier when offered food or out to eat with friends. They might also say they are trying to lose weight but do not go into detail about the extremes of how they are doing this.

A person with an eating disorder often does not see themselves the way others see them. They may not see themselves as underweight when they are dangerously thin.

However, friends and family may notice comments about "feeling fat" or other statements showing low self-esteem, poor body image, and an obsession with becoming smaller. Those with anorexia may obsessively weigh themselves, and as they lose more and more weight, it can become apparent to those around them that they are not eating much.

According to NIMH, some warning signs of developing anorexia include:

- *Extremely restricted eating*
- *Extreme thinness (emaciation)*
- *A relentless pursuit of thinness and unwillingness to maintain a normal or healthy weight*
- *Intense fear of gaining weight*
- *Distorted body image, a self-esteem that is heavily influenced by perceptions of body weight and shape, or a denial of the seriousness of low body weight*[5]

Another behavior someone battling anorexia may engage in is excessive exercise. They may begin running farther and farther distances in an effort to burn extra calories, visit the gym more than once a day, or take hours of exercise classes in a row. From the outside, this can look like a newly adopted fitness habit, but those with anorexia take their fitness too far.

In addition to causing mental distress, excessive exercise can add to the physical problems someone with anorexia faces. Girls who exercise too much may change their menstrual cycle or cause it to stop entirely. In *The Truth About Eating Disorders*, Gerri Kramer wrote, "People who exercise compulsively may experience dehydration, broken bones, torn ligaments, joint problems, osteoporosis, and even heart and kidney failure. A healthy amount of exercise builds muscle, but too much actually destroys the muscle."[6] In addition to overexercising, someone with anorexia may take diet pills or laxatives and may even throw up after they eat.

The Mayo Clinic lists a number of behavioral warning signs that someone is developing or has

Exercising can be a good thing, but it can also be taken too far.

developed an eating disorder such as anorexia. These include:

- *Skipping meals or making excuses for not eating*
- *Adopting an overly restrictive vegetarian diet*
- *Excessive focus on healthy eating*
- *Making own meals rather than eating what the family eats*
- *Withdrawing from normal social activities*
- *Persistent worry or complaining about being fat and talk of losing weight*
- *Frequent checking in the mirror for perceived flaws*
- *Expressing depression, disgust, shame or guilt about eating habits*

TOO MUCH OF A GOOD THING

For most people, moving their body every day or several times a week is healthy. Some people enjoy training for long-distance cycling or running events. Others want to see how much weight they can lift. Most just want to keep their body healthy. However, for someone with an eating disorder, exercise is just one more way to deprive their body of needed calories. Their food and workout become parts of a transactional relationship—the more they eat, the more they need to move. They may also add more exercise to their routine because they find their food restriction unsustainable. Writer and eating disorder recovery advocate Tabitha Farrar wrote on her blog that when she was going through anorexia, her doctor never asked how much she was exercising, only how much she was eating: "I *was* eating, but that was on the condition that I exercised for over six hours a day. In a sense, my anorexia was hiding in plain sight."[1]

She described the intense fear she felt from not being able to exercise as much as she felt she needed to. Farrar recalled that her need to negate calories extended even beyond formal exercise:

> *The compulsion to move continued to exist in practically every move I made. Taking the longer route. Walking rather than taking the car. Getting up and down to fetch things when eating a meal. Never sitting. Always having to stand. Fidgeting. I was not allowed to sit down during the day. If I had to (say a car ride or a situation where I could not stand) I would have to "make it right" by eating less that day.*[2]

After realizing she needed to stop exercising to get well, it took Farrar two years to actually stop. She acknowledges that the role exercise played in her anorexia was the hardest part for her to overcome. For her, the only way to stop the excessive exercise cycle was to quit "cold turkey," or all at once—something she recommends to others facing a similar struggle.

1. Tabitha Farrar, "Exercise and Anorexia: The Case for Cold Turkey," Tabitha Farrar, May 2017. tabithafarrar.com/2017/05/exercise-anorexia-case-cold-turkey/.

2. Farrar, "Exercise and Anorexia."

- *Eating in secret*[7]

These behaviors may only be obvious to a friend or family member who is specifically on the lookout for warning signs, especially since many people with anorexia try to engage in their behavior without anyone knowing. Over time, though, physical symptoms of anorexia arise. A very low body weight is one obvious symptom, although some people may try to hide this by wearing layers of clothing or baggy clothing. Someone with anorexia may complain about being very tired, cold, or constipated. Their skin can take on a yellowish color and begin to look dry. Their hair and nails will become brittle and break easily. Some people with anorexia grow fine hairs called lanugo all over their body. The body does this to try to keep its temperature up in the absence of calories to burn for heat. These are only the physical problems that can be seen; less visible, internal medical issues are also caused by anorexia.

SYMPTOMS OF BULIMIA AND BED

Actress Candace Cameron Bure did not struggle with disordered eating until she was an adult, despite growing up on television. When she married her husband, a professional hockey player, she moved away from all her family and friends. She said she lost a sense of who she was:

> *I sat lonely so many nights not knowing what to do with myself. But there was always one friend that was always there, that was so readily available anytime I wanted, and that for me was food ... It became a very destructive relationship, and it was one that really caught me off guard. I got into a cycle of binge eating and feeling such guilt and shame for that, that I would start purging. And without even knowing, it soon just took over to a point where you feel such a loss of control.*[8]

Her father eventually found out about her behavior, and Bure was able to stop. However, a few years later, she started bingeing and purging again. This time, she got professional help and has successfully recovered.

Like anorexia, the behaviors that are signs of bulimia often happen in secret and are accompanied by feelings of shame. Binge eating behaviors, such as those Bure described, might only happen when a person is alone. They can be triggered in someone with bulimia by a stressful situation, feeling hunger after trying to restrict food intake, or feeling bad

People with bulimia spend a lot of time in the bathroom, especially right after they have eaten.

about one's self, especially in terms of body size. Following a binge, someone with bulimia will force themselves to purge the calories they have taken in by throwing up, taking many laxatives, fasting, or exercising excessively. It is important to remember that bulimia and binge eating disorder share the component of a binge, but in BED, the sufferer will not engage in purging behavior on a regular basis like someone with bulimia.

Sometimes it is a dentist who first notices some of the telltale signs of bulimia, such as damaged teeth and gums. When a person vomits frequently, stomach acid wears away the enamel of their teeth and causes them to turn brown. Frequent vomiting also causes sores in the throat and mouth. It may cause swelling of the salivary glands in the cheeks (a condition commonly called "chipmunk cheeks"), and the voice of a person with chronic bulimia may become hoarse.

Another clue to behaviors of someone with bulimia is the appearance of bruises, sores, or calluses on the knuckles or fingers. These occur when the person sticks their fingers down their throat to make themselves vomit and the fingers scrape against the teeth.

Friends and family can watch for some warning signs that a loved one might be suffering from bulimia in addition to calluses or sores on hands and a hoarse voice. They may hear someone suffering from bulimia be overly critical of their body shape and weight. According to the website Eating Disorder Hope, those who have developed bulimia may isolate themselves and tend to eat in private. They may hide food. These behaviors are also true of BED sufferers. Most obviously, someone suffering from bulimia will often go to the bathroom during a meal or right after they have eaten.

The NEDA lists several more warning signs of bulimia:

- *In general, behaviors and attitudes indicate that weight loss, dieting, and control of food are becoming primary concerns*
- *Evidence of binge eating, including disappearance of large amounts of food in short periods of time or lots of empty wrappers and containers indicating consumption of large amounts of food*
- *Evidence of purging behaviors, including frequent trips to the bathroom after meals, signs and/or smells of vomiting, presence of wrappers or packages of laxatives or diuretics*
- *Appears uncomfortable eating around others*
- *Develops food rituals (e.g. eats only a particular food or food group [e.g. condiments], excessive chewing, doesn't allow foods to touch)*
- *Skips meals or takes small portions of food at regular meals*
- *Any new practice with food or fad diets, including cutting out entire food groups (no sugar, no carbs, no dairy, vegetarianism/veganism)*
- *Fear of eating in public or with others*
- *Steals or hoards food in strange places*
- *Drinks excessive amounts of water or non-caloric beverages*
- *Uses excessive amounts of mouthwash, mints, and gum*
- *Maintains excessive, rigid exercise regimen—despite weather, fatigue, illness, or injury—due to the need to "burn off" calories*

- *Creates lifestyle schedules or rituals to make time for binge-and-purge sessions*
- *Withdraws from usual friends and activities*
- *Looks bloated from fluid retention*
- *Extreme mood swings*[9]

TEMPORARY RELIEF

The rituals and secrecy of the behaviors of anorexia and bulimia may sound exhausting to someone not dealing with these disorders. However, there is evidence that these behaviors make sufferers feel good temporarily. Some medical professionals believe those who purge may experience a rush of endorphins, which are the feel-good hormones the body creates. However, that feeling does not last.

As the warning signs show, many behaviors and warning signs of anorexia and bulimia are similar. Additionally, according to the testimony of many medical experts, incidences of anorexia and bulimia are frequently interlinked; for instance, a patient with bulimia often has a history of anorexia. When the anorexia is supposedly cured, the eating disorder sometimes reemerges as bulimia. This means someone with an eating disorder may receive several diagnoses, as their behavior may be consistent with multiple disorders.

GENDER DIFFERENCES

When anorexia and bulimia are developing, it can be very difficult for loved ones to notice that their friend or family member is engaging in disordered behaviors. Spotting warning signs of an eating disorder may be even more difficult if the sufferer is a man. This is likely due to the societal assumption that people with eating disorders, especially

NORMAL VS. ABNORMAL DIETS

When a person suddenly decides to be vegetarian or vegan, it can be a sign of an eating disorder. However, it is important to note that this is not always the case. Many people who are vegetarian or vegan eat enough, get a variety of nutrients, and maintain a healthy body while doing so.

One way to tell whether following one of these diets is a warning sign is the reason people give for their decision. Vegetarians typically do not eat meat, while vegans typically do not eat anything that comes from animals at all, including cheese, honey, and eggs. Someone whose diet change is a result of an eating disorder may be attracted to these diets because it is an easy way to cut out food groups without being questioned about why they are eating less than normal. They may also tell people they are doing it to lose weight, and they eat noticeably less than they used to.

However, there are many reasons why people who do not have an eating disorder may choose to become vegetarian or vegan. One is for their general health. Doctors caution that eating too much meat can be unhealthy, so some people choose to cut it out completely. These people pay attention to their nutritional needs and eat enough to get full. Another reason is concern for the environment, including climate change and animal welfare. Demand for large amounts of meat, especially beef, contributes to climate change because more animals are needed to meet that demand. Large cattle farms lead to the cutting down of trees to make room for huge herds of cows to graze. The cows' burps produce methane, a gas that traps heat in the atmosphere and contributes to global warming. Many animals that are raised for their meat, especially chickens and sheep, are also not treated well. They live in small cages and have a high risk of getting sick. Some vegetarians and vegans cut out animal products to spare animals from these conditions.

anorexia and bulimia, are women. Although it is true that many people with eating disorders are women, men can also have a poor body image and need for control that they try to combat with the behaviors associated with anorexia and bulimia. The essential features of eating disorders are the same regardless of gender. Still, there are some warning signs that tend to be unique to men.

First, men may use excessive exercise for other reasons than to lose weight, although some also use it for that. They may develop an unhealthy obsession with gaining muscle mass—getting "shredded" or "ripped"—or with becoming a better athlete. All of this may be partly to attain a certain body type that society tells them is the "ideal," just like the women who excessively exercise and diet. The ideal body type for men, however, happens to be muscular rather than small and slim. A clear obsession with "getting big" can be a warning sign that a man is developing anorexia or bulimia. Sometimes, these behaviors are called "bigorexia," although this is not a medical term.

Some men dealing with an eating disorder also control their food intake and sometimes try to eat less and less. Others may be incredibly focused on the kinds of foods they are eating and make a strict plan for their intake, often including a lot of protein for muscle-building purposes. This kind of obsession with a certain nutrient, especially protein (and sometimes fiber), is also observed in women, especially in recent years.

Male disordered eating behaviors can sometimes provide clear warning signs that something is wrong, but they tend to be explained away by practices that are culturally acceptable. For example, binge eating affects many men, but they may be praised for the amount of food they can eat. According to the American Addictions Centers, "Some people believe that men, if given the opportunity, will sit down and eat everything they can find. This is a cultural expectation, and it makes [bingeing] at least familiar, if not accepted, behavior for all men."[10]

Men might believe the opposite to be true too:

If it is assumed that lazy, unappealing men eat anything they can eat in great amounts, men with anorexia or bulimia who have very strict rules

BED is less likely to be spotted in men because of society's idea that men normally eat excessive amounts of food.

about what they can and cannot eat might be praised for that behavior. It might seem as though they are pushing back against a negative stereotype, and they might get recognition, not concern, for the food choices they make.[11]

Excessive exercise is also more accepted for men than for women, as society's expectations for men revolve around being strong.

Because of these cultural ideas, men are less likely to have someone notice their behavior. Like those around them, they may not even see

AN INCREASED RISK

For many years, transgender and nonbinary people have been ignored in research, including on topics such as how eating disorders affect them. While this has changed in recent years, studies are still limited. However, the research that has been done indicates that both groups are at higher risk for developing eating disorders. This is especially true of trans people.

In 2018, The Trevor Project—a mental health resource for LGBTQ+ people—partnered with the NEDA to survey 1,034 LGBTQ+ people between the ages of 13 and 24. Of those survey respondents, 51 percent said they had been diagnosed with an eating disorder at one point in their life. For trans respondents who identified as straight, that number rose to 71 percent. The most common eating disorder in this population was anorexia.

As with cisgender people, the causes of eating disorders are complex; there is no single cause. However, dissatisfaction with their body is a big risk factor for a person developing an eating disorder. Trans people often experience body dysmorphia, which is a disorder in which a person feels shame or disgust about the way their body looks and behaves. Experts suggest that trans people may be more at risk for developing anorexia because their body dysmorphia leads them to seek out ways to change their body.

The ways society views gender play into this problem. A trans woman may start dieting or over-exercising to achieve a more "feminine" appearance, while a trans man may restrict his food intake so that his body weight gets low enough to stop his period or make his breasts smaller. Affordable and available gender-affirming care, including hormone therapy and tools such as chest binders, as well as creating places where trans people feel safe to be themselves may help reduce this risk.

their behaviors as disordered. However, their body dissatisfaction is consistent with anyone who has anorexia or bulimia. It can have an incredibly negative effect on their overall mental health:

> *If he cannot talk about the way he feels about his body, or if he does not feel as though he can discuss the foods he either craves or ignores, even though these are thoughts that consume him, he*

> *may not feel as though he can have an authentic relationship. He may withdraw from his relationships altogether, or he may lash out at the few people who are trying to help him. As his isolation grows, his need to medicate with food may grow yet stronger.*[12]

Understanding warning signs can help those with eating disorders recognize they need help or can cause those around them to see that help should be offered. Regardless of someone's gender, warning signs should not be ignored. They are crucial to notice for diagnosis to occur and treatment to follow.

Many people with an eating disorder only receive treatment after being formally diagnosed with it by a doctor. A patient must meet the criteria listed in the *DSM-5* in order to be given such a diagnosis.

ANOREXIA IN THE *DSM-5*

Diagnostic criteria are conditions that must be present for someone to be diagnosed with a disorder. They are extremely important because some disorders look similar to each other and because sometimes people show certain symptoms of a disorder without actually having it. For example, if someone is traveling a long distance and does not have enough money to buy food at the airport, they may not eat a lot that day, but this does not mean they have anorexia. The diagnostic criteria for anorexia are:

> *A. Restriction of energy intake relative to requirements, leading to a significantly low body weight in the context of age, sex, developmental trajectory, and physical health. Significantly low weight is defined as a weight that is less*

than minimally normal or, for children and adolescents, less than that minimally expected.

B. *Intense fear of gaining weight or of becoming fat, or persistent behavior that interferes with weight gain, even though at a significantly low weight.*

C. *Disturbance in the way in which one's body weight or shape is experienced, undue influence of body weight or shape on self-evaluation, or persistent lack of recognition of the seriousness of the current low body weight.*[13]

To be diagnosed with restricting type anorexia, a person must not have binged or purged in at least three months; instead, they must have achieved their unusually low weight "primarily through dieting, fasting, and/or excessive exercise."[14] To be diagnosed with binge eating/purging type, the person must have engaged in more than one episode of this behavior.

To diagnose the severity of a person's anorexia, doctors take into account how far below the normal body mass index (BMI) range a person is. BMI is based on a calculation of the person's height and weight. While many experts have noted flaws in using BMI as an indicator of overall health, it is a useful way for doctors to determine how far below a standard healthy weight a person with anorexia is.

BULIMIA AND BED IN THE *DSM-5*

People with bulimia regularly engage in episodes of binge eating. This is defined in the *DSM* as:

1. *Eating, in a discrete period of time (e.g., within any 2-hour period), an amount of food that is definitely larger than what most individuals*

would eat in a similar period of time under similar circumstances.

2. *A sense of lack of control over eating during the episode (e.g., a feeling that one cannot stop eating or control what or how much one is eating).*[15]

These criteria are the same for diagnosing BED. Other criteria for binge eating include eating more quickly than normal, eating until feeling uncomfortably full, eating large amounts of food despite not feeling hungry, feeling embarrassed about the amount of food one is eating, and feeling disgusted, depressed, or guilty after a binge. Unlike anorexia or bulimia, a person's appearance is not part of the diagnostic criteria for BED.

After binge eating, people with bulimia compensate for the large amount of food they have consumed by purging. This is an important part of the diagnosis because it distinguishes bulimia from BED. Furthermore, to diagnose bulimia, the bingeing and purging must occur together at least once a week for three months, and the person must be excessively concerned about their body image. To distinguish bulimia from binge eating/purging type anorexia, behaviors related to bulimia must not "occur exclusively during episodes of anorexia nervosa."[16]

Because people with bulimia tend to maintain a more average body weight than people with anorexia, the criteria for determining severity is different. Instead of going by BMI, the severity of bulimia is judged by the number of times a person purges per week. For example, a mild case involves one to three episodes of purging per week, while an extreme case involves 14 or more per week. However, when determining the level of severity, doctors may also take into account how much the symptoms of the disorder affect the person's life.

A CHANGING RESOURCE

Since the first edition of the *DSM* was published, the diagnostic categories and criteria for many mental health issues, including eating disorders, have changed. In the most recent edition, the *DSM-5*, some significant updates to the eating disorder criteria were made. Previously, amenorrhea, or the loss of the menstrual cycle, was a criterion for anorexia nervosa. This has been removed, allowing the diagnosis to be more inclusive. Since everyone's body is different, some women keep having a period even when they lose a lot of weight. Before the change to the diagnostic criteria, these women could not be diagnosed with anorexia even if they had all the other symptoms. The removal of amenorrhea from the criteria also makes the diagnosis more inclusive of men who never had a period to begin with as well as for trans women. No longer is there a weight requirement for an anorexia diagnosis either. Instead, the *DSM-5* asks that health care professionals evaluate a person's weight in the context of their age, health, sex, and overall development.

The criteria for bulimia nervosa also changed slightly from older *DSM* versions. First, the required frequency of purge behavior for diagnosis changed to once a week for three months instead of twice a week for three months. It also eliminated subtypes of bulimia. In addition, BED became a separate disorder with its own criteria for diagnosis.

These changes were made to make the criteria easier for doctors and other health-care professionals to understand and use. They were also meant to decrease the number of patients diagnosed

Doctors stay up to date on the changing diagnostic criteria in the *DSM*, but with so many diseases and disorders, it's hard to stay on top of them all. Some doctors specialize in eating disorders, so they are more knowledgeable. Your doctor may refer you to a specialist if you have an eating disorder.

with less specific eating disorders, which are more difficult to treat in a standard way.

GETTING INFORMED

Doctors and other medical professionals spend time ruling out other illnesses or disorders that could affect a person's weight, physical health, and mental health before someone is given a diagnosis of an eating disorder. For example, patients with hyperthyroidism can have weight loss, amenorrhea, or problems absorbing food—but they do not have disordered eating behavior. In these cases, the patient's symptoms are caused when their thyroid gland, which plays a role in regulating weight, does not function as it should. In order to determine whether someone meets the criteria of the *DSM*, doctors often interview their patients showing symptoms of anorexia or bulimia. They may also use rating tests such as the Eating Attitudes Test, Eating Disorders Inventory, or Body Shape Questionnaire to aid in a confident diagnosis. The answers to the questions on these rating tools are self-reported by the patient.

The Eating Attitudes Test lists statements for a responder to consider, such as, "I avoid eating when I am hungry."[17] Then, the responder chooses "always," "usually," "often," "sometimes," "rarely," or "never." Certain responses to certain statements give a score of 0 to 3. When a trained mental health professional evaluates the responder's answers, they will calculate a total number. Higher numbers generally indicate that the person who took the test needs further evaluation for eating disorders.

CATCHING OTHER CASES

In the *DSM-IV*, a major category of eating disorders was called eating disorders not otherwise specified. This catchall diagnosis included those who did not properly meet the criteria for a specific disorder. It was the most common eating disorder diagnosis.

In the *DSM-5*, this classification was changed to other specified feeding or eating disorder (OSFED) or unspecified feeding or eating disorder (UFED). Someone diagnosed with OSFED might have many features of anorexia except the extreme weight loss. They may not meet the threshold of time required for a bulimia or BED diagnosis because they have engaged in bingeing or purging behaviors for less than three months or less frequently than weekly. Others may purge without bingeing. Similarly, a person diagnosed with UFED meets some criteria of an eating disorder (or other *DSM* feeding disorder category) but not all.

These two classifications are important since many people with disordered eating behaviors do not necessarily fit into the narrow categories of anorexia, bulimia, and BED, but they still need a way to get professional help. Some mental health professionals believe eating disorders occur on a spectrum and believe diagnoses should reflect that. Until that time, these categories can help more people get treatment they need.

Those suffering from eating disorders do not always look like they have a problem, especially in Western cultures in which thinness, concern about diet, and exercising are admired. A person's culture has a large effect on what they value in themselves and others. This influence can play a large role in the start of an eating disorder.

Like many other medical problems, eating disorders have multiple complicated causes. Sarah Haight—a fashion writer whose work has appeared in *Vogue*, *Teen Vogue*, *Women's Wear Daily*, and *W* magazine—has discussed the causes of her eating disorder:

> *Anorexia is one of the most difficult illnesses to trace the origins of: Its roots are tangled, and the delicate unbinding of each contributing factor can be done only once the patient has truly agreed to get help. In my case, the disease was the product of a complicated mélange [combination] of emotional pain, perfectionism, societal pressure, and genetic bad luck. Every anorexic has a narrative of where things started to go awry [wrong].*[18]

Haight's assessment sums up the difficulty of eating disorders: There is no single specific cause to find, fix, or stop. A mix of genetic and biological factors, trauma, stress, and cultural expectations is often to blame. In addition, many who suffer from anorexia and bulimia have other mental health issues that can be part of the cause of—or be worsened by—an eating disorder. They must receive treatment for those along with the eating disorder, which can make recovery even harder. Researchers continue to study individuals with eating disorders to find things sufferers have in common, but the causes are often a complex, individual mix of emotions, environment, and biology.

THE ROLE OF GENETICS

A number of research studies have provided evidence that eating disorders can run in families. In fact, someone who has a family member with an eating disorder is 7 to 12 times more likely to also develop an eating disorder than someone without a family history of one. Children who are born to parents who have had anorexia at some point are 10 times more likely to develop anorexia themselves than the general population is.

Ira Sacker, a leader in the field of eating disorders, said that when he first began treating patients with eating disorders, he did not pay much attention to the eating patterns of their parents. He was surprised to discover that many parents admitted they, too, had experienced some kind of disordered eating in their past. He now believes eating disorders have a genetic component, meaning there may be some aspect—researchers are unsure exactly what, since there is no specific "eating disorder gene"—that gets passed down from parent to child. Sacker said:

> *Having a family history of eating disorder, addictions, and obsessive-compulsive behavior doesn't guarantee that someone will develop an eating disorder. It does suggest, however, that awareness of the possibility needs to be present, just as there needs to be an awareness of a family history of, say, breast cancer or diabetes.*[19]

A study at the Medical College of Virginia at Virginia Commonwealth University focused on identical and fraternal twins. Identical twins develop from the same egg, so they have almost the exact same genes. Fraternal twins develop at the same time from two different eggs, so their genes are less similar. The researchers found that identical twins had a much higher incidence of eating disorders than fraternal twins did, so the scientists concluded that heredity plays a role in eating disorders.

Studies done on twins have shown that eating disorders have both genetic and environmental causes.

The researchers also pointed out that environmental and emotional factors might make twins particularly susceptible to the development of an eating disorder.

Brain chemistry may also play a role in causing someone to develop anorexia or bulimia. Studies on this topic often consider the role of serotonin, a chemical used by nerve cells. It affects the digestive system and has been found to play a role in hunger and food cravings. Christopher G. Fairburn, an expert who has done extensive research on eating disorders, said:

> *Interestingly, dieting has been shown to affect certain chemical transmitters in the brain, particularly serotonin, and this effect is more pronounced [noticeable] in women than in men. Since serotonin is thought to play a role in the normal control of eating as well as in food selection, this finding is intriguing … Put simply, it seems that an abnormality in brain serotonin function may put people at risk of developing bulimia nervosa and that dieting in women may exaggerate [increase] this risk.*[20]

Professor of health education Mark Kittleson pointed out that serotonin is one of the neurotransmitters, or brain chemicals, that give a person a sense of physical and emotional fulfillment. He said, "Serotonin, in particular, sends the message that you feel full and have had enough to eat. Researchers have found that acutely ill patients suffering from anorexia and bulimia have significantly lower levels of serotonin."[21]

Dopamine, a chemical made by the body that takes part in the emotional and pleasure centers of the brain, has also been connected with anorexia and bulimia. Research has found that those with anorexia likely make too much dopamine. Bulimia, on the other hand, is characterized by someone not making enough dopamine, and some experts believe that bingeing may encourage a dopamine release by the brain.

SOCIAL FACTORS

Biology alone does not determine a person's fate. Although a young man or woman might have a family member with an eating disorder, that does not guarantee that they are also destined to

Trauma makes a person feel out of control. After a traumatic event, such as a tornado, a person may develop an eating disorder as a way to try to regain control of their body and life.

develop one. In fact, one of the greatest risk factors for developing any eating disorder is engaging in diet behavior. The Mayo Clinic states that it is possible that dieting to lose weight may actually cause the brain to change in those who are already at risk. Another risk factor that could push someone with a genetic predisposition toward an eating disorder is stress. The stress could be as common as moving, starting at a new school, or having a fight with a family member or friend.

However, a stressor could be far more serious and continue to affect a person long after it is over. An event that has occurred that has a strong negative effect on someone is called trauma. Trauma includes any kind of abuse, such as physical, emotional, or sexual abuse. It also includes things such as being part of a terrible car accident or natural disaster. Trauma could also occur after witnessing something disturbing, such as a death.

FATPHOBIA

In many cultures, especially Western ones, being thin has become one of the biggest beauty ideals. Phrases such as "you can never be too rich or too thin" reinforce the idea that thinness is the ultimate goal. In fact, some people have come to believe that being thin proves that a person is morally good. Fat people are often seen as lazy and overly focused on eating large amounts of food, while thin people are often seen as hardworking and goal-oriented. This is because many people have the mistaken idea that anyone who eats less and exercises more can easily become very thin. In reality, everyone's body is different, and body size is not an indicator of overall health, a person's general habits, or morality.

The dislike of and discrimination against people in larger bodies is called "fatphobia." It can harm fat and thin people alike. Fat people are sometimes encouraged to develop eating disorders; if they start out trying to eat less and exercise more and remain overweight, they may be told they are not doing enough and be pressured to restrict their diet further and over-exercise, eventually pushing them into anorexia. When thin people open up about their disordered eating habits and the distress those habits have caused them, they may be told that those habits clearly worked for them and thus were good. Even doctors can be blinded by their fatphobia and encourage disordered eating habits. In reality, disordered eating is a serious problem that causes severe mental and physical health problems. No one should be encouraged to harm themselves just to conform to someone else's idea of what the "right" body looks like. Experts say the emphasis should be on a person's overall health, not what their body looks like or how much they weigh.

According to the Center for Eating Disorders at Sheppard Pratt:

> *Survivors of trauma often struggle with shame, guilt, body dissatisfaction and a feeling of a lack of control. The eating disorder may become the individual's attempt to regain control or cope with these intense emotions. In some cases, the eating disorder is an expression of self-harm or misdirected self-punishment for the trauma.*[22]

OTHER DISORDERS

Many people who suffer from eating disorders have other mental health issues to deal with too. These comorbidities—any two or more disorders that occur at the same time—make treating eating disorders more difficult, but they can also serve as early red flags to health-care providers that an individual may be at a higher risk of developing an eating disorder. Often, there is no way to know

COMMON COMORBIDITIES

DEPRESSION loss of interest in previously enjoyed activities, feelings of sadness, loss of energy, feelings of worthlessness	**BIPOLAR DISORDER** alternating periods of high mood, energy, and activity (manic) and low energy, mood, and activity (depressive)	**PANIC AND ANXIETY DISORDERS** greater than usual feelings of nervousness or fear about an event, place, or action
POST-TRAUMATIC STRESS DISORDER (PTSD) occurs following a traumatic event; reliving bad memories, feeling anxious or edgy, having trouble sleeping	**OBSESSIVE-COMPULSIVE DISORDER (OCD)** thoughts that repeat over and over, thoughts or ideas that are not wanted arising, the need to repeat actions many times	**OBSESSIVE-COMPULSIVE PERSONALITY DISORDER** obsession with things being neat and orderly, need to feel in control of all situations, inability to make decisions quickly
BORDERLINE PERSONALITY DISORDER mood swings, problems sustaining personal relationships, feelings of uncertainty about self	**SLEEP DISORDER** problems with getting not enough sleep or too much; problems with getting quality sleep	**SUBSTANCE ABUSE OR DEPENDENCE** using drugs or alcohol in a harmful way

These are just a few of the most common comorbidities of people who suffer from eating disorders.

which mental health issue developed first.

One study found that 97 percent of women being treated at an inpatient hospital for an eating disorder had a comorbidity. Some of these diagnoses, such as depression, anxiety, and abuse of drugs or alcohol, occur across eating disorders and at fairly high rates. Depression is reported as the most common comorbidity among those diagnosed with an eating disorder. Other comorbidities of eating disorders include post-traumatic stress disorder (PTSD), borderline personality disorder, and sleep disorders.

Obsessive-compulsive disorder (OCD) seems to be particularly common among those with anorexia, reinforcing the idea that these sufferers seek perfection, order, control, and ways to cope with distress. The abuse of drugs—especially alcohol—is more likely among those with bulimia.

PRESSURE FROM OTHERS

Society often plays a large role in how people feel about themselves. From actors and athletes to the selectively shared images on social media, it is easy for people to find others to compare themselves to. Those who are at risk for eating disorders may be even more affected by these outside influences. They provide a body type to aspire to, even if that body type is unrealistic for the average person to achieve. Size 00 models and celebrities are constantly splashed across the media. Heroes and heroines onscreen are generally beautiful and thin. Characters with larger bodies may be either villains or supportive best friends, but they are not often the stars.

These characterizations can have serious consequences. Anne Becker, a professor at Harvard Medical School, published a study describing what happened in Fiji, a small island nation in the Pacific Ocean, before and after television arrived. Before American television arrived, Fijians considered the ideal body to be curvy, round, and soft. After three years of watching TV shows from the United States, teenage girls showed serious signs of eating disorders. The Harvard study found that Fijian teens who watched three or more nights of TV per week were more likely to consider themselves too fat. They told investigators they had begun dieting and vomiting to control their weight. The study, begun in the mid-1990s, reported that by 2007, 45 percent of girls on the main island of Fiji said they had engaged in purging behaviors.

Although culture affects how people see themselves and others, concern with body image may begin at home with innocent remarks from parents who warn against eating too much and becoming fat. Other relatives might make a comment about someone being chubby or about what or how much they eat. Siblings and classmates might come up with hurtful nicknames. Some cultures, such as certain Asian cultures, may be more prone to making these comments than others. Children and teens may begin engaging in disordered eating behavior to uphold the cultural expectations of their family.

Professor of psychology Susan Mendelsohn widens the net of influence even further:

> *Home and school are not the only breeding grounds for body image derailment. What about the candy store clerk who "cuts you off" after a few candy bars, the local [boys] who shout insults from their car windows as they pass, or the beloved neighbor who has a nickname for everyone, usually to reflect the opposite of how they appear. The town giant is "Tiny," the city octogenarian [80-year-old] is*

"Youngun," and you're "Slim," nicknamed with a know-it-all grin.[23]

PRESSURE ON ATHLETES

Successful athletes are under heavy pressure. They set high goals for themselves. They are often more determined and more disciplined than the average individual. The competitive sports environment adds to the pressure. Anxiety about their performances and negative self-judgment can lead to excessive concern about their bodies—and to eating disorders.

Although any athlete can develop an eating disorder, people in activities that emphasize leanness for performance and appearance are at much greater risk. Wrestlers and jockeys who have to meet rigid weight requirements may develop unhealthy ways of losing or gaining weight. Swimming, diving, dancing, track, and gymnastics have traditionally called for strong, light bodies.

In an article written for Vanderbilt University, Ana Cintado explained one reason gymnasts are vulnerable to eating disorders:

Anorexia often strikes young women who try to evade [avoid] the natural process of becoming adults and who use excessive measures to maintain a thin and girlish figure—the exact description of what today's female gymnast must accomplish to stay competitive at the highest levels. For these athletes, the onset of womanhood is their biggest fear because it means developing hips or breasts that might hinder their performance. Thus, starving themselves offers the most convenient solution to their problem.[24]

Many female athletes have begun to speak out about their struggles with eating disorders. In

2018, Victoria Garrick—a libero on the women's volleyball team at the University of Southern California—talked about her struggle when she joined the team as a freshman. She did not want to work out or eat the way she was instructed to for fear her body would change. She said, "Female athletes have pressure from society and Instagram to look one way and then we have pressure from

Both male and female athletes are under a lot of pressure to get stronger, faster, and sometimes thinner.

our team and the sports world to look another way. As my body started to get bigger, I could hear my mind start to say 'Don't eat carbs, don't eat this.'"[25] She found herself turning to food to cope with uncomfortable emotions regarding her body and the lifestyle pressures of Division I athletics. Soon, her mental health began to suffer as well. She ended up taking a break from playing volleyball to help heal her body and mental state, but she noted, "It's hard to take time off from competing for an injury that people can't see."[26]

PRESSURE FROM THE INTERNET

Although much blame has been directed at the fashion and entertainment media for promoting images and behavior that lead to eating disorders, the influence of peer-driven social media may be even more dangerous. Pro-ana (pro-anorexia) and pro-mia (pro-bulimia) content was a major part of social media platforms such as Instagram and Tumblr in the 2010s. This often included content known as "thinspiration," which brought together those who wanted to share tips on being "better" at their eating disorder and offer motivation to keep going down those paths. For a long time, searching for a hashtag such as #thinspiration was all it took. However, in 2012, Instagram and Tumblr both banned content that promoted any self-harm—including eating disorder behaviors.

Many applauded this decision, but as BuzzFeed News pointed out in a 2016 article, the ban may have made the problem worse. Hashtags that were clearly related to thinspiration were no longer allowed on Instagram, but motivated users came up with many variations on these words in order to continue sharing and taking in content they wanted. In fact, a 2015 study by the Georgia Institute of Technology

THE INTERNET IS NOT REAL LIFE

In 2024, Nicholas Perry—better known by his YouTube handle, Nikocado Avocado—shocked his fans by revealing that he had lost 250 pounds (113 kg) seemingly overnight. The YouTuber, who weighed about 411 pounds (186 kg) at his heaviest, had become famous for eating large amounts of food in his videos. In his reveal video, Perry explained that he had been on a weight loss journey for the previous two years. He had hidden it by uploading pre-recorded videos of himself during that time. Perry said the reason he did this was to show people that what they see on the internet is not always what is happening in real life, noting the times viewers had insulted his appearance. Many comments expressed concern for his health, which is a move experts have labeled "concern trolling." This is when a person pretends to care about a fat person's health to disguise their own fatphobia. Their true goal is to bully the fat person into losing weight because they dislike fat people in general.

Other social media personalities sometimes claim that their thinness is natural or comes from a strict diet and exercise routine, but are later revealed to be suffering from an eating disorder. Eugenia Cooney, who posts on YouTube and TikTok, denied for years that she had anorexia, in spite of the fact that her followers could see her getting dangerously thin. In 2016, thousands of people signed a petition to ban her from YouTube, stating that she was a bad influence on impressionable young fans. YouTube never followed through with the ban, and Cooney denied having anorexia. However, in 2019, she admitted that she did have an eating disorder and talked about her road to recovery. Viewers praised her for her honesty and willingness to get help. Cooney later relapsed, and since that time, she has celebrated her thinness while making no mention of her eating disorder. Many viewers suspect that she enjoys reading comments about how thin she is, which may have fueled her relapse and stopped her from seeking help again.

said the ban made engagement with eating disorder content greater on Instagram than it had been previously.

In the 2020s, a new social media trend came into the spotlight, and it reminded many people, especially women, of the pro-ana and pro-mia content of the decade before. "SkinnyTok" emerged on platforms such as TikTok and Instagram, with influencers offering tips on how to eat less and encouraging negative self-talk as a kind of "motivation" strategy. Experts have cautioned against the rise of this kind of content, with many saying that it promotes eating disorders.

Researchers have offered ways to combat the ever-growing groups of those with eating disorders on platforms such as these, including marking certain posts with a content advisory that contains a link to the NEDA website or redirecting someone who searches for eating disorder content directly to NEDA. However, others say these efforts could further alienate those suffering from eating disorders rather than encourage them to get help.

ARE EATING DISORDERS CONTAGIOUS?

Eating disorders are not contagious in the same way as measles or the flu, but the idea of having an eating disorder can be catching. Seeing websites, groups, or even news stories about someone with anorexia, bulimia, or another eating disorder can lead to someone developing an eating disorder themselves.

The idea of "catching" or "spreading" eating disorders has been around for many years. British psychologist Gerald Russell, who wrote the first paper describing bulimia as a separate illness from anorexia, has even said that he takes "full responsibility" for the disorder's spread by publishing that paper: "There was a common language for it. And knowledge spreads very quickly."[27] Once bulimia nervosa was part of the *DSM*, more papers came out about this "new" eating disorder. The information filtered down into women's magazines such as *Better Homes and Gardens*, which is how such a widespread audience learned about it. According to an article on *The Cut*, "Psychologists studying the developmental psychopathology of eating disorders have led dozens of controlled experiments finding a near-perfect link between mass media and eating disorder symptoms."[28]

Sometimes an eating disorder such as anorexia is shown to spread throughout a group. At least three members of the British musical group the Spice Girls, who were popular in the late 1990s and early 2000s, have admitted to suffering from eating disorders. Geri Halliwell (Ginger Spice) said she developed eating disorders while living with the other Spice Girls. She felt she was fat compared to other band members and developed bulimia while trying to lose weight. Victoria Beckham (Posh Spice) said that Geri encouraged her and Melanie Chisholm (Sporty Spice) to take up running and to eat liquid meals. Eventually, Beckham started to binge eat; at one point, she ate 10 bowls of cereal in one sitting. Chisholm starved herself and exercised excessively. She admitted in 2017, "I started to restrict my food to a point where I was just … eating fruit and vegetables."[29]

The causes of anorexia and bulimia are complex. Compounded by cultural pressure, societal expectations, risk factors, and comorbidities, it may seem very difficult to treat the mental health aspects of eating disorders—and it is. However, the medical consequences of an eating disorder are also complicated and often must be addressed before any psychiatric work is done.

HEALTH PROBLEMS

Anorexia remained a hidden disorder for many years, with sufferers often succeeding in keeping their problems a secret. Those closest to sufferers might have realized something was wrong, but with diet culture and extreme thinness becoming more popular, strangers were likely to just see a person whose diet was succeeding. However, when Karen Carpenter died in 1983, the world suddenly knew what the word "anorexia" meant. Even scarier, everyone now knew the deadly consequences of eating disorders. Carpenter had been seeking treatment for her years of dieting, laxative use, and use of medication that sped up her metabolism. For her, it was help sought too late. Her heart and digestive system were already weak. The Los Angeles coroner reported her cause of death as "heartbeat irregularities brought on by chemical imbalances associated with anorexia nervosa."[30]

Death is the worst outcome of anorexia and bulimia. However, even before a fatal event such as the cardiac arrest of Karen Carpenter, there are many other troubling physical complications that can affect an eating disorder sufferer.

A SLIPPERY SLOPE

Although research shows that dieting is a serious risk factor for developing an eating disorder,

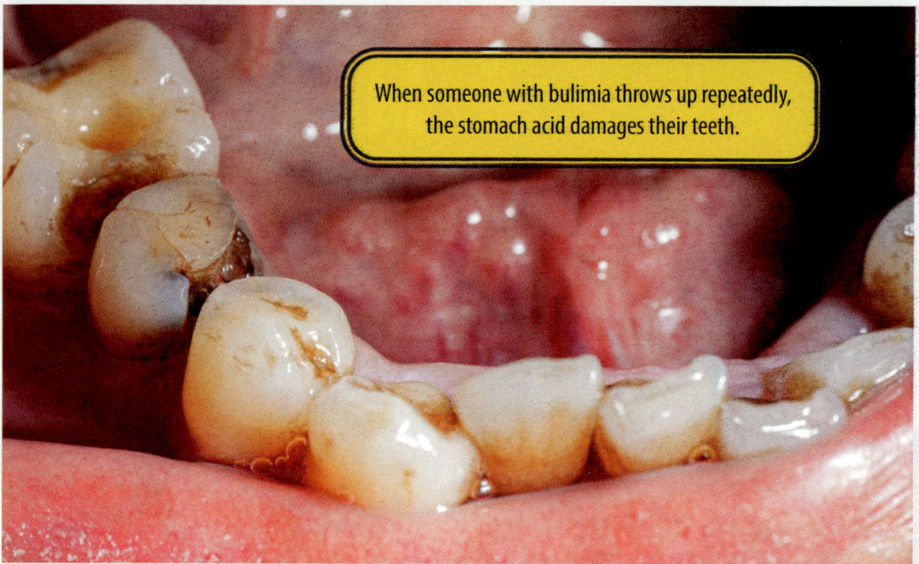

When someone with bulimia throws up repeatedly, the stomach acid damages their teeth.

many people likely do not see skipping a meal here or there as a big deal. Similarly, they may exercise excessively after a big meal once in a while. However, these behaviors are a slippery slope. They can lead to avoiding eating altogether or spending all their free time trying to "burn off" whatever they have eaten. The eating disorder does not have to be incredibly severe for the body to respond. Over time, medical issues and serious physical problems can arise from eating disorders at any stage of severity.

For example, bulimia can cause dental problems. Vomit contains a lot of acid, and this acid can damage the teeth, leading to tooth decay and sensitive teeth. It can also cause harm to the esophagus and intestines. Those who are purging in this way tend to have an irritated, sore throat that will not go away, and they can develop a long-term problem such as acid reflux. In fact, the acid may wear away at the esophagus and stomach so much that either one could rupture.

Those with eating disorders may have many other problems with their digestive system. Both restriction of calories and vomiting can cause slow digestion and constipation. The muscles of the intestines, like all the muscles in the body, need nutrients to function. Without proper nutrition, they can weaken and be unable to properly move food through the digestive tract. Not eating enough may also stop bowel movements because there simply is not enough food in the system to eliminate it. Furthermore, if laxatives are abused, the body may eventually not be able to have a bowel movement without them.

Purging as well as excessive laxative use can cause dehydration or an electrolyte imbalance, which means there is too much or too little sodium, calcium, potassium, or other minerals in the body. Potassium, for example, helps the heart beat and the muscles work correctly. If there is too little of it in the body, someone might experience irregular heartbeats, eventually leading to heart failure. Electrolyte imbalances and dehydration affect the brain too. They can lead to seizures or even strokes.

The brain also suffers from lack of nutrition. It needs sources of fats to keep the layer of fat around neurons (nerve cells) healthy and strong. Without it, this layer can be damaged, and the person's hands, feet, and limbs may tingle or go numb.

Fats also contribute to the creation of hormones throughout the body. Those who are not eating enough fat or calories in general can cause their hormone levels to fall, causing irregularity of menstruation or amenorrhea in people assigned female at birth (AFABs).

Taking in too few calories causes other body tissues to break down too. Since the body needs fuel, it starts to break itself down to use for energy. This often starts with muscle—and because the heart is primarily made of muscle, this breakdown can be particularly problematic. It can cause blood pressure and heart rate to drop as the heart cannot pump the way it needs to.

An eating disorder such as anorexia or bulimia can affect the body down to the cellular level. The body's metabolic rate falls with a lack of food to burn and use for energy. This often makes eating disorder sufferers cold and can even cause them to develop hypothermia, which is when the internal body temperature drops too low. They may stop making enough of some kinds of blood cells. Anemia occurs when someone does not have enough red blood cells or is not taking in enough iron. It makes a person feel tired, weak, and short of breath. Poor nutrition also decreases the number of white blood cells in the blood, meaning there are fewer to fight disease and infection.

EFFECTS OVER TIME

There are long-term health issues that can come about from anorexia and bulimia. Low levels of certain sex hormones can cause osteopenia and osteoporosis, which are a weakening and loss of bone in the body. Once bone loss has begun, it cannot be reversed, only managed. For people who have these conditions, the risk of broken bones remains higher for the rest of their lives. Additionally, irregularities in the menstrual cycle can cause a person to have trouble getting pregnant. Women who have suffered from anorexia have higher miscarriage rates and lower rates of carrying a baby to term. Women with bulimia are at risk of a relapse if they do get pregnant.

People who binge as part of their eating disorder often do so on foods that are considered very tasty, such as those high in sugar, fat, and salt. Even if these foods are purged by vomiting or using laxatives, parts of them can remain in the body to be digested. Over time, intake of these foods can disrupt how the body deals with the hormone insulin, which regulates blood sugar. Type II diabetes is a possible result of years of binges of these kinds of foods.

It is also important to remember that the physical issues that are caused by eating disorders only get worse the longer someone restricts, purges, or otherwise engages in eating disorder behaviors. Given enough time, many of these issues—particularly those having to do with the brain and heart—can cause death.

ANOREXIA AFFECTS YOUR WHOLE BODY

brain and nerves
trouble concentrating, fear of gaining weight, sadness, mood swings, irritabilty, bad memory, fainting, changes in brain chemistry

hair
thins and gets brittle

heart
low blood pressure, slow heart rate, palpitations, heart failure

muscles and bones
weak muscles, swollen joints, fractures, osteoporosis

kidneys
kidney stones, kidney failure

blood
anemia and other blood problems

intestines
constipation, bloating

hormones
periods stop, bone loss, problems growing, fertility issues; if pregnant, higher risk for miscarriage, emergency C-section, baby with low birth weight, and postpartum depression

skin
bruising easily, dry skin, growth of fine hair on body, yellow skin, brittle nails, feeling cold

essential minerals
low potassium, magnesium, and sodium

Left untreated, eating disorders such as anorexia can truly harm the whole body.

DEATH RATES

Anorexia has the highest mortality, or death, rate of all psychiatric disorders. One study published in 2016 found that, when compared with peers who did not have eating disorders, those with anorexia were five times more likely to die by the time the study was completed. Another study found that someone with anorexia who has binged and purged in the past was more likely to die. Some researchers have reported that bulimia and BED seem to have a lower mortality rate than anorexia, but they still have serious health consequences.

Death rates for eating disorders for the general population are hard to know for sure for a few reasons. The percentage of those who died often depends on the severity of the eating disorders in the population studied. Some studies do not have enough participants to give rates that can be generalized well. Other researchers look at many studies and form a conclusion based on these without collecting new data. Most of all, sometimes eating disorders are not reported as the cause of a death. Instead, another health problem will be reported as the cause, even if that problem was caused by an eating disorder. For example, if anorexia weakened someone's heart, the cause of death might be listed as heart failure.

About 30 to 40 percent of eating disorder sufferers engage in self-harm of some kind. This increases their likelihood of death through accidental injury. These behaviors can also escalate into thoughts of suicide.

Compared to the general population, people with eating disorders such as anorexia and bulimia are much more likely to die by suicide. Studies have shown that around 17 percent of people diagnosed with anorexia attempt suicide. In fact, about one in every five deaths attributed to anorexia is a suicide. Michael Rollin, a psychiatrist at the Eating Disorder Center of Denver, Colorado, gave *Social Work Today* some insight as to why the suicide rate is so high:

It [anorexia] not only takes over their behavior but their physical health and the content of their minds. One of the biggest frustrations of people with eating disorders is that it's what they spend their day thinking about, planning around, and essentially doing all day long. It hijacks their lives and in that way, they often feel like they have no respite [relief].[31]

Researchers in one small study found that in these cases, the sufferer showed a genuine wish to

DYING FOR HER CAREER

Christy Henrich was a world-class American gymnast. She made the U.S. national gymnastics team, and in 1988, placed ninth at the Olympic Trials. In 1989, she won the silver medal in the all-around U.S. National Championships. She represented the United States at the World Championships in Stuttgart, Germany, placing fourth with the American team. One balance beam leap that she originated was named after her, and it is still included in the Code of Points for artistic gymnastics.

When a judge at the international meet in Stuttgart told Christy she needed to lose weight, she took the comment to heart, and a five-year battle with her body began. She developed anorexia, and her alarmed family eventually forced her to enter a hospital. She went through periods of recovery, relapses, and numerous treatments, but it was too late: The damage done to her body was too severe. Eight days after her 22nd birthday, Christy died of multiple organ failure.

Her death caused a spotlight to be turned on the problem of eating disorders in gymnasts. Kim Arnold, a U.S. team member in the 1990s, said, "There was a lot of eating and purging. You used to see how little you can eat today and still get through a workout. We used to see how many meals we could miss before we had to eat again."[1]

According to Ron Thompson, an eating disorder specialist who has consulted with the Indiana University athletic department, the gymnasts' youth and their driven personalities plus the competitive environment puts them at high risk for eating disorders. "These kids are so mentally tough, so willing to do anything the coach says will make them a better athlete," Thompson said. "They're perfectionists so continuing to train on broken bones and having eating disorders is normal behavior to them."[2]

1. Quoted in Scott M. Reid, "Emphasis on Thin Is a Heavy Burden," *GYM Media Report*, January 16, 2005. www.gymmedia.com/FORUM/agforum/05_01_henrich_e.htm.

2. Quoted in Reid, "Emphasis on Thin Is a Heavy Burden."

die. The suicides studied were carried out in ways that would be difficult to prevent and did not have anything to do with starvation, restricting food, or other characteristic eating disorder behaviors. A licensed clinical social worker at the Renfrew Center of New York, Connie Quinn, said this would make sense: "The self-loathing associated with anorexia is so punishing that it wouldn't seem extraordinary to me that extreme measures might be taken to end that suffering."[32]

TURNING TO EXPERTS

Someone suffering from bulimia or anorexia may not be able to see beyond their eating disorder to understand the great danger they are in. A friend, family member, teacher, or doctor might be the person to bring up health issues they see, whether physical or mental. For some, that might be enough to seek help on their own. They might opt for outpatient treatment, which means living at home but seeing a therapist, dietician, and other health professionals to begin working through their disordered behaviors. However, many sufferers may feel angry or deny they have a problem. They may not willingly participate in outpatient services for their eating disorder. In some cases, they may need to be checked into an inpatient hospital specializing in eating disorders. This process generally starts when someone with anorexia or bulimia has a serious medical issue and they are checked into a hospital to deal with it. Very low blood pressure, electrolyte imbalances, and low core body temperature are all reasons for someone with an eating disorder to be seen in a hospital. Once they are medically stable, they will go through a physical and psychiatric evaluation to see if their case is serious enough for inpatient treatment.

EATING DISORDERS AND TRAUMA

Music artist Kesha told *Rolling Stone* in 2017 about some of her eating disorder struggles. She felt pressure to look a certain way in order to keep her career in music going—largely from her producer, Dr. Luke, who constantly told Kesha she was fat and pressured her to lose weight. She alleged that he also forced her to take certain drugs and sexually abused her.

The emotional and physical abuse Kesha said she experienced from Dr. Luke took a toll on her. She developed bulimia, and the weight loss that stemmed from this disorder got her positive attention—which she found confusing. She said, "I was slowly, slowly starving myself. And the worse I got and the sicker I got, the better a lot of people around me were saying that I looked. They would just be like, 'Oh, my gosh, keep doing whatever you're doing! You look so beautiful, so stunning.'"[1]

Kesha showed strength by turning to others for help. Her music after recovery has reflected her growth.

Eventually, Kesha turned to her mother for help. Her mom sent her to a rehabilitation center to recover, where she met with someone to help her with nutrition and relearned how to eat healthily. After she was released from the center, she refused to allow Dr. Luke to have influence over her any longer. She also continued to pay attention to her physical health. Even when she is on tour, she said, "I always have three meal breaks, 'cause being in recovery, I need to have time to sit and eat a meal."[2]

1. Quoted in Brian Hiatt, "The Liberation of Kesha," *Rolling Stone*, October 4. 2017. www.rollingstone.com/music/music-features/the-liberation-of-kesha-123984/.

2. Quoted in B.S, "Lawsuits, Bulimia and a Near-Death Experience: Kesha's Neverending Comebacks," *El País US Edition*, June 22, 2023.

A decline in weight despite trying other outpatient interventions for the eating disorder or a weight that is less than about 75 percent of a healthy weight are two reasons inpatient treatment might be considered. Additionally, having suicidal thoughts or severe depression or being unable to take care of oneself also may cause someone to be placed in an inpatient treatment facility.

When someone is admitted to an inpatient facility specializing in eating disorders, their immediate needs are met first. This may include further medical intervention to keep them alive and medically stable. In a hospital specializing in eating disorders, a person has many health professionals to help, day and night. These include a medical doctor who will treat the physical complications of their eating disorder. Patients will also see a therapist who specializes in eating disorders to begin the difficult work of stabilizing their mental health. They will begin to work with a dietician or other nutrition professional to start monitoring how much and what the patient eats. If the patient refuses to eat enough—or at all—a tube may be inserted into their nose and down their throat to feed them directly. This intensive refeeding is sometimes also necessary for eating disorder sufferers who are too weak to feed themselves yet.

For many, a stay at an inpatient treatment facility is an important step toward recovery. However, it is very expensive to stay in one of these facilities, so most people do not stay very long. When they are released, most continue with outpatient treatment. Treatment for anorexia and bulimia is multifaceted, and although the road to recovery is long, it is possible to reach the destination of health—both mental and physical.

CHAPTER FIVE

TREATING EATING DISORDERS

Because every person with an eating disorder is different, there is no quick and easy treatment that works for everyone. Instead, treating anorexia and bulimia is much like working on a very difficult puzzle. First, doctors need to put the pieces together for a diagnosis. Next, the underlying causes of the eating disorder need to be explored. Does this patient have anxiety or a family history of eating disorders? Have they endured some kind of trauma? In addition, family, friends, and medical professionals must convince a patient with anorexia or bulimia that they need help. Some people who have eating disorders refuse to believe their behavior can have serious effects and do not seek help until it is too late to save their lives. Others feel their lives are worthless and that they do not deserve help. Only when the person with the eating disorder is willing to participate can a treatment plan begin to take shape.

The final picture of eating disorder diagnosis and treatment looks different for every patient. While one person may do well in group therapy alone, another may need medication and nutrition help. Few people are able to fully recover on their own. The process of recovering from an eating disorder is challenging—and it may last for the rest of a person's life. However, it is worth the effort.

SETTING GOALS

The very first goal of any treatment of an eating disorder, including anorexia and bulimia, is restoring the patient's health. For those who are hospitalized, immediate health issues, such as very low blood pressure, are handled first. All those with eating disorders, whether their treatment starts in a hospital or not, are evaluated for health issues that need to be treated right away. Then, their team of medical professionals begins to work toward bettering their nutritional status. For example, someone with anorexia who has been eating very few calories will slowly increase calorie intake. For many, this will include adding in supplements such as vitamins to make sure the body is getting the micronutrients it has not been getting.

Over time, eating more helps sufferers reach a healthy weight. However, adding in more food can be difficult physically and should be closely monitored. Those in treatment may experience bloating or constipation. This step can be difficult psychologically as well. Feelings of anxiety, frustration, and stress about eating and gaining weight are likely to come up. That is why another treatment goal is to work toward a healthy relationship with eating, food, and the body. Many organizations and noted eating disorder specialists believe that both the physical and emotional problems underlying anorexia and bulimia have to be treated, but exploring the psychological problems that led to the development of the disorder can only begin once serious medical problems have been treated and weight restoration has begun.

Many factors have to be considered when working out the type of treatment that will be most likely to succeed with a particular patient. These include the person's age, their overall physical

A PERSONAL APPROACH

Many therapists who are now working in the field of eating disorders have battled these diseases themselves. Lindsey Hall recovered from bulimia and went on to write several books on eating disorders with her husband, Leigh Cohn. Hall was the first person who recovered from bulimia to appear on national television. Both she and her husband have lectured extensively on eating disorders and served as officers of nonprofit eating disorder associations. They are well-known authorities worldwide in the field of eating disorders. Their books have been translated into Japanese, Chinese, Italian, and other languages. Hall's understanding of eating disorders has been acquired through long years of close association with these disorders. She has written:

> *In a perfect world, free from eating disorders, all people would appreciate that love and self-esteem are their birthright regardless of shape or weight. Families, aware of the causes and consequences of eating disorders, would be a constant source of communication and sharing ... Food would be a symbol of life rather than a tool for abuse. In other words, people would be allowed to be themselves without conforming to tight-fitting roles based on artificial limits.*[1]

1. Lindsey Hall and Leigh Cohn, *Bulimia: A Guide to Recovery*. Carlsbad, CA: Gürze, 1999, p. 73.

condition, how quickly the patient has been losing weight, the length of their illness, and information about previous treatments. Also important is how willing the patient is to cooperate in exploring the psychological problems underlying the disease.

TALKING TO A THERAPIST

When an eating disorder has been going on for some time, professional help is generally necessary to repair the psychological damage it has done and to stop it from getting worse. Psychotherapy is a form of treatment that involves discussions between a therapist and a single patient or a group of patients. It is also known as talk therapy, counseling, or psychosocial therapy. Individual psychological treatment is most common for adults, especially those who live alone. Many types of individual therapy are available. A type of talk therapy called cognitive behavioral therapy (CBT) helps the patient identify unhealthy, negative beliefs and behaviors and replace them with healthy, positive ones. It is based on the idea that a person's thoughts, not other people or situations, determine how a person behaves. CBT has proven to be especially beneficial in treating bulimia. It is also used to treat anorexia.

A therapy known as dissonance-based (DB) has shown good results in treating eating disorders. In this type of therapy, people examine the messages society is sending them about their bodies—especially the need to be thin in order to be beautiful and worthy of love—and learn how

Therapists are trained to help people take charge of their mental health.

to identify the problems with those messages. The idea is that once people understand more about the negative messages they are being sent, they will be better able to resist them. DB sessions can take place either one-on-one with a therapist or in a group setting.

Interpersonal therapy focuses on the person's current relationships with other people. The goal of this therapy is to improve the person's skills in relating to others, including family, friends, and coworkers. The patient learns how to evaluate the way they interact with others and develop strategies for dealing with relationships and communication problems.

Family therapy is especially important for children or young adults who still live at home. It can help concerned family members learn the best ways to help the patient. It can also resolve family conflicts and uncover family problems that may have been at the root of the eating disorder. Author Steven Levenkron said family therapy can be a powerful tool for bringing about rapid change in the relationships that contribute to eating disorders: "[Family therapy] is a setting where often the 'unsayable' (at home) can now be said because a 'referee' is present; a setting where a family can use the therapist as a teacher and role model who can step back, analyze the conflict, and resolve it."[33]

A form of family therapy developed by researchers at the Maudsley Hospital in London, England, has received worldwide attention. It focuses on patients who are acutely ill with anorexia. In this method, the family is seen as the most important resource at the therapist's disposal. The family is not blamed for the illness. Instead, the Maudsley therapist tries to empower the family to assume the responsibility for nurturing their ill child back to

THERAPY INVOLVING ANIMALS

Some therapists are turning to innovative kinds of treatment. David Herzog, an internationally renowned expert on eating disorders, recommends using pets in treating patients. Touch and trust, he says, are very important in the healing process.

Caroline Knapp, one of his patients, has written a memoir, *Pack of Two: The Intricate Bond Between People and Dogs*. In this book, Knapp relates her experience with anorexia and the way in which her pets help her stay well. She wrote, "Put a leash in my hand, put Lucille [her dog] by my side, and something happens, something magical, something clicks inside, as though some key piece of me, missing for years, has suddenly slid into place, and I know I'll be okay."[1]

The use of horses in residential programs is growing in popularity. Remuda Ranch in Arizona was one of the first to use equine therapy in treating eating disorders. Each patient rides two or three times a week on a particular horse that is assigned to them. Sharon Simpson, director of Remuda Ranch, said the bond that develops between horse and rider creates a sense of unconditional acceptance that many patients have never experienced before. "Perfection," said Simpson, "does not enter the relationship. The horse is a living breathing animal, and because of that, he can be unpredictable, just like life is unpredictable."[2]

Animals can provide people with love, companionship, and responsibility for another living thing.

1. Quoted in Aimee Liu, *Gaining*. New York, NY: Grand Central, 2008, p. 132.

2. Quoted in Liu, *Gaining*, p. 134.

health. Despite the fact that this may be frightening to the family, the therapist encourages them with warm acceptance and gives them the expertise to change their child's destructive behavior.

Group psychotherapy is often used together with individual psychotherapy in both inpatient and outpatient settings. Different groups have different goals. Some groups focus on food, eating, body image, interpersonal skills, or job training. Other groups focus on understanding the psychological factors that may have led to the development of the disorder. The participants learn that they are not alone in their struggles. Their interactions (under the guidance of a therapist) include both supporting and confronting each other.

Sharing experiences in a group can be effective in reducing guilt, shame, and feelings of isolation. Group discussions can also lead to insights about strategies for recovery. There are potential downsides to group therapy; for instance, the youngest members may learn new ways to lose weight or, as sometimes happens in a group of people with anorexia, some may compete to be the thinnest person. However, on the whole, most experts agree that group therapy is generally more beneficial than harmful in treating eating disorders.

MEDICAL INTERVENTION

When psychotherapy is not enough to help a patient with anorexia or bulimia, medications may be prescribed. According to the NIMH, antidepressants, antipsychotics, and mood-stabilizing medications can be helpful in treating eating disorders and their comorbidities, such as depression and anxiety. Someone suffering from an eating disorder who also experiences another mental health condition will work closely with their medical team to determine the right kind and dosage of medication. This process that can take patience and time.

Antidepressants can be used to help treat depression and anxiety while a patient is also undergoing therapy. According to the Cleveland Clinic, medication can help someone reduce their binges. The most commonly prescribed type of antidepressant is a selective serotonin reuptake inhibitor (SSRI), which stops the brain from reabsorbing too much serotonin after it is initially released. The

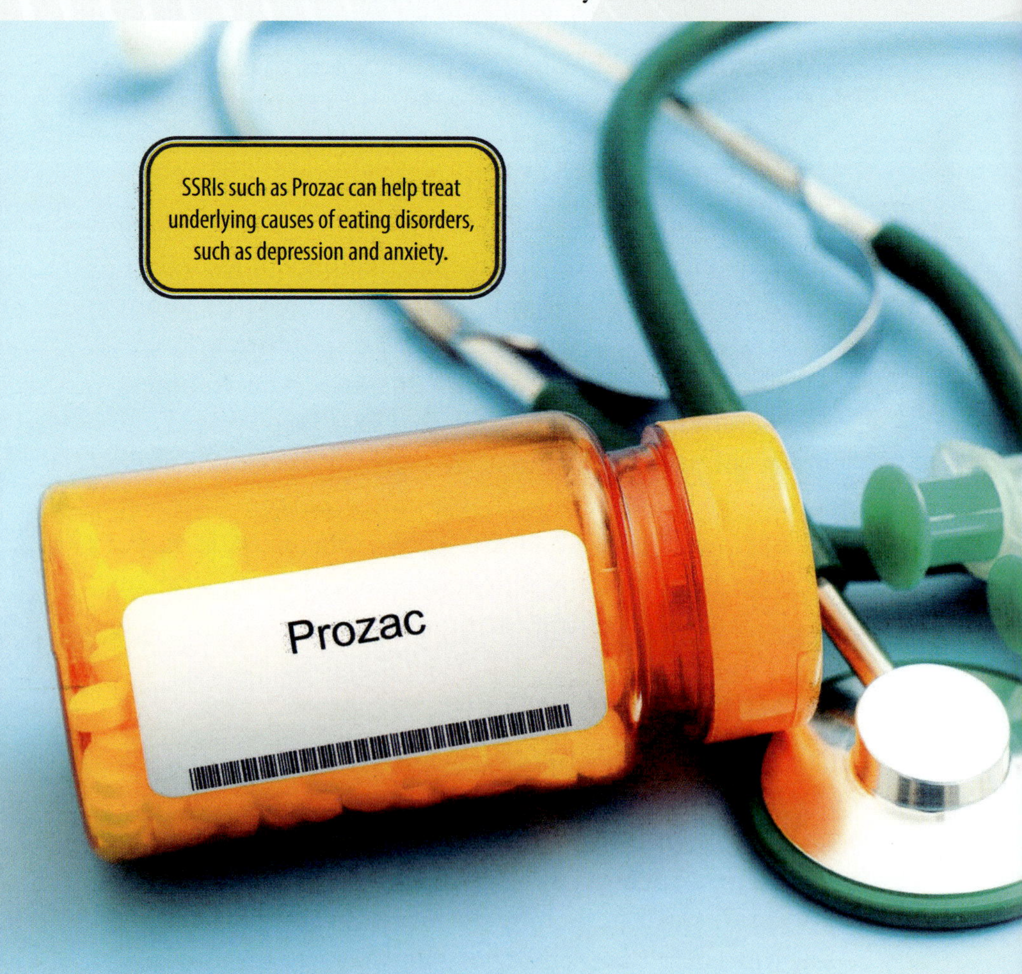

SSRIs such as Prozac can help treat underlying causes of eating disorders, such as depression and anxiety.

U.S. Food and Drug Administration (FDA) has approved Prozac (fluoxetine) to treat bulimia, but other medications in its class of SSRIs have also been shown to be helpful. SSRIs seem to be less successful in treating anorexia, but another kind of antidepressant called a tricyclic antidepressant may be more helpful in this area. Tricyclics increase the level of neurotransmitters such as serotonin in the brain.

Anxiety may be one of the contributing causes of eating disorders, and it is likely to increase as the patient worries about undergoing treatment for the disease. Antianxiety drugs can be prescribed to help patients feel calmer. However, the body develops a tolerance to them, so they become less effective over time.

As happens with many effective but powerful drugs, medications used to help patients with anorexia and bulimia can have troublesome side effects. These may include tiredness, confusion, and low blood pressure. Therefore, it is important that patients taking them have ongoing medical supervision. Experts agree that medication alone is rarely a solution to recovery from an eating disorder. However, when combined with psychotherapy, medication can be helpful.

FINDING SUPPORT FROM PEERS

Support groups can be life-saving when their goal is to help members overcome their eating disorders and maintain healthy lifestyles. On the other hand, support groups that encourage members to think of their diseases as lifestyles can be deadly. In these groups, members learn ways to support their illnesses and share tricks to hide them from others. With a little research, reliable support groups can be found, and most of them are free. Some support groups focus on behaviors that are related to eating disorders. Others deal with underlying emotional issues as well as behaviors.

Going to a support group for the first time can be a scary experience—especially for a person who has been hiding their disease. Jennie, who suffered from bulimia, described her first experience of attending a support group recommended by her doctor: "I didn't think I was going to be able to walk through the door. My whole body was shaking … Even though the atmosphere was casual, it was hard to open up at first."[34] Although her story was different from the others' in the group, as she listened to them talk, she realized they had things in common. "If they were going to make an effort to get over this," Jennie said, "I had no excuse not to try as well."[35]

Joining a support group can help people with eating disorders connect with others who understand what they are going through.

THE ROAD TO RECOVERY

When eating disorder sufferers accept the fact that their disorder is controlling their lives and become willing to make necessary changes, they can hope to recover. Experts agree that no one with a severe eating disorder finds healing to be a neat, orderly, or predictable process. Slipping back into old hurtful habits of behavior during treatment as well as relapses after treatment ends are common. Commenting on celebrities who have been "cured" of an eating disorder, Ira Sacker said, "Actors and models appearing on talk shows make it sound as if getting over an eating disorder is quick and easy, but the reality is very different. Every step of the way is paved with speed bumps, and progress is slow and uneven, with plenty of setbacks."[36]

Michael Strober, director of the Eating Disorder Program at the University of California, Los Angeles (UCLA), Neuropsychiatric Institute, has treated eating disorders for more than 30 years. At UCLA, he said, patients with anorexia and bulimia are considered recovered "when they maintain a healthy weight and no longer obsessively count calories, binge or purge or manically exercise."[37] For women, regaining their menstrual cycle is a key sign that they are recovering too.

However, even years later, these recovered patients show abnormally high rates of anxiety and obsessive thinking, especially perfectionism. "The solution," Strober said, "is not to eliminate these traits but to learn to manage them. So in treatment we try to move patients to a new framework, to enable them to accept growth and change."[38]

It is also vitally important for them to learn to recognize and avoid triggers that may cause a recurrence of their symptoms.

SLIPPING INTO OLD HABITS

Despite stories of celebrities who go to rehab centers for a few weeks and emerge cured of their eating disorders, the road to recovery is seldom short or straight. The website Anorexia Nervosa & Related Eating Disorders (ANRED) estimated that about 60 percent of people who have eating disorders fully recover. Of the remaining 40 percent, about half will partially recover and half will deal with their eating disorder for life.

Recovery involves not only physical progress but also emotional healing. After many years of treating patients with eating disorders, Sacker put the stumbling blocks for patients into four categories: slips, lapses, relapses, and collapses.

Slips are disordered thoughts that originate in the patient's mind. A patient with anorexia might have negative thoughts about eating. A patient with bulimia might think about what they have eaten and about ways to purge it from their body. If the patient hides these kinds of disordered, negative thoughts from their therapist, the thoughts may build up until they lead to a lapse.

A lapse occurs when the patient acts on their disordered thinking. It is generally limited and brief—for example, skipping only one meal—but it is scary for the patients and may make them feel as if they are failures. The therapist will try to make the patient understand that lapses are common and are to be expected on the way to recovery.

A relapse is far more serious. It is a return to the eating behavior that made the patient sick. "The difference between a lapse and relapse," Sacker said, "is the difference between a stumble and a bad fall. When you stumble, you can catch yourself in the midst of it; when you fall, you can't stop yourself at all."[39]

With proper treatment, the relapse may be turned around. However, if it is not caught and stopped immediately, it may become a collapse—a full-blown return of the original eating disorder behavior. In fact, it may become an even more intense form of the disorder or even another type of eating disorder. Patients sometimes go through more than one cycle of relapse and collapse. They may require medical attention to repair physical damage to their bodies or psychiatric care and medication to prevent suicide.

FACING OBSTACLES

Many people who have suffered from eating disorders are now happy, healthy individuals. They may have had lapses and relapses on the way to recovery. Eventually, however, they learned ways to cope with the obsessive feelings that still return from time to time. This is especially necessary in times of stress.

Nicole, who survived bulimia, said her recovery was neither easy nor completely secure. However, during treatment, she learned strategies for overcoming the impulses that might trigger a relapse. "There are times even now," she said, "five years later—that I find myself in a food panic. But now, whenever I feel the urge to chow and purge an entire cake, I stop myself and ask, 'Why? Am I really hungry? Or is it because I'm anxious or feeling pressured by something else?'"[40]

Each time she makes it safely through the panic attack, her self-confidence grows. She said, "Now I know I'm in charge. Every time I beat that feeling, it's like saying, 'This is my body and my life.'"[41]

Joyce Maynard is a writer who became obsessed with her weight and body size in her late teens. She trained herself to monitor every bite of food that entered her mouth. If she let herself slip and eat a piece of bread or a piece of chocolate, she felt self-hatred and disgust. She convinced herself that food was her enemy.

Then, she entered into a relationship with a man who tried to tell her what to eat and how much to eat. She rebelled and started to sneak food. She would binge and then vomit to get rid of the calories. She no longer knew how to eat like a normal person. "I knew only two conditions," she said, "total denial, total indulgence."[42] After becoming a mother, she gradually and painfully learned to eat normally.

Thirty years later, the wiring in her brain caused by her disordered eating is still there. She has compared herself to an alcoholic who has been sober for 30 years and still speaks of herself as "recovering." She said, "All these years later ... I can tell you the exact number of calories in a cashew."[43] When she imagines herself getting the flu and throwing up for a couple of days, she hears an internal voice, as if from a radio station, whispering in her ear, "'Oh good, I bet I'll drop four pounds.' I no longer expect," Maynard continued, "this voice will ever be silenced entirely. All I can do is take it in, and change the station."[44]

EARLY IDENTIFICATION

It is nearly impossible to know who will develop an eating disorder. Medical professionals can identify those who are at high risk for developing one, but even that can be hard to know without a detailed family history, honest conversations about dieting, and careful monitoring of a person's body weight. This means that prevention of eating disorders in all populations should be the goal.

The Mayo Clinic suggests ways for parents to prevent eating disorders in their children, but they

Food is a central part of life. Everyone deserves to be able to eat it without feeling shame or fear.

can be applied to everyone. First, the organization advises avoiding dieting. Instead, people should learn to enjoy food and understand how a balanced diet helps their health, both physical and mental. Next, if a person sees portrayals of bodies on TV or online that trouble them or cause disturbing thoughts, it is important for them to talk to a trusted friend or adult. Finally, everyone should work to maintain a healthy body image. This can be difficult if a person's friends participate in body shaming of themselves or others.

Young adults can be the voice of reason by reminding everyone that body shapes and sizes vary. They can also avoid criticizing their own body, instead replacing negative thoughts such as 'My legs are big and ugly' with neutral or positive ones such as 'My legs are strong and I am a fast runner.'

This practice will improve their own body image as well as their peers'.

There are many organizations that work to promote a healthy body image and push back against the influence of diet culture, and anyone can become part of one of them. By helping to change the conversation surrounding food, bodies, and self-worth, they are helping to prevent eating disorders.

Finally, the first line of defense against eating disorders is friends and family. If someone notices any warning signs of anorexia, bulimia, or any other eating disorder, they should say something. It may be easier for them to enlist the help of a guidance counselor, coach, or parent. A loved one's concern could be the reason someone gets the help they need before their disorder goes too far.

Eating disorders are complex mental disorders that millions of people around the world suffer from. However, each of these individuals feels alone in their disorder. By doing further research to help understand different types of eating disorders, medical professionals and—more importantly—the family and friends of these sufferers can better make these individuals feel seen, heard, and helped.

NOTES

CHAPTER ONE: WHAT ARE EATING DISORDERS?

1. "What Are Eating Disorders?," NEDA, accessed on September 28, 2018. www.nationaleatingdisorders.org/what-are-eating-disorders.
2. Liliana Dell'Osso, et al., "Historical Evolution of the Concept of Anorexia Nervosa and Relationships with Orthorexia Nervosa, Autism, and Obsessive-Compulsive Spectrum," National Institutes of Health, July 7, 2016. www.ncbi.nlm.nih.gov/pmc/articles/PMC4939998/.
3. Caroline Hopkins, "Eating Disorders Among Teens More Severe than Ever," NBC News, April 29, 2023. https://www.nbcnews.com/health/health-news/eating-disorders-anorexia-bulimia-are-severe-ever-rcna80745.
4. Quoted in Nick Wilson, "An Eating Disorder Nearly Derailed His MLB Dream. Now This Former Catcher Is Raising Awareness," *The Tribune*, August 8, 2018. www.sanluisobispo.com/news/health-and-medicine/article216205995.html.

CHAPTER TWO: SIGNS AND SYMPTOMS

5. "Eating Disorders," National Institute of Mental Health, accessed on September 28, 2018. www.nimh.nih.gov/health/topics/eating-disorders/index.shtml.

6. Quoted in Mark J. Kittleson, ed., *The Truth About Eating Disorders*. New York, NY: Facts On File, 2005, p. 70.
7. Mayo Clinic Staff, "Eating Disorders," Mayo Clinic, February 22, 2108. www.mayoclinic.org/diseases-conditions/eating-disorders/symptoms-causes/syc-20353603.
8. Quoted in Gabrielle Olya, "Candace Cameron Bure on Her Struggles with Bulimia: 'It Was Never About the Weight, It Was an Emotional Issue,'" *People*, May 4, 2016. people.com/bodies/candace-cameron-bure-opens-up-about-her-struggles-with-an-eating-disorder/.
9. "Bulimia Nervosa," NEDA, accessed on September 28, 2018. www.nationaleatingdisorders.org/learn/by-eating-disorder/bulimia.
10. "Male Eating Disorder Awareness and Treatment," American Addiction Centers, last updated July 31, 2018. americanaddictioncenters.org/male-eating-disorders/.
11. "Male Eating Disorder Awareness and Treatment," American Addiction Centers.
12. "Male Eating Disorder Awareness and Treatment," American Addiction Centers.
13. Brian C. Harrington, et al., "Initial Evaluation, Diagnosis, and Treatment of Anorexia Nervosa and Bulimia Nervosa," *American Family Physician*, January 1, 2015. www.aafp.org/afp/2015/0101/p46.html.
14. Harrington, et al., "Initial Evaluation, Diagnosis, and Treatment of Anorexia Nervosa and Bulimia Nervosa."
15. Harrington, et al., "Initial Evaluation, Diagnosis, and Treatment of Anorexia Nervosa and Bulimia Nervosa."

16. Harrington, et al., "Initial Evaluation, Diagnosis, and Treatment of Anorexia Nervosa and Bulimia Nervosa."

17. Psych Central Researchers, "Eating Attitudes Test," Psych Cental, last updated July 25, 2018. psychcentral.com/quizzes/eating-attitudes-test/.

CHAPTER THREE: COMPLEX CAUSES

18. Quoted in Kate Taylor, ed., *Going Hungry*. New York, NY: Anchor, 2008, pp. 181–182.

19. Ira Sacker, *Regaining Your Self*. New York, NY: Hyperion, 2007, p. 162.

20. Christopher G. Fairburn, *Overcoming Binge Eating*. New York, NY: Guilford, 1995, p. 74.

21. Kittleson, ed., *The Truth About Eating Disorders*, p. 45.

22. "What Causes An Eating Disorder?," The Center for Eating Disorders at Sheppard Pratt, accessed on October 1, 2018. eatingdisorder.org/eating-disorder-information/underlying-causes/.

23. Susan Mendelsohn, *It's Not About the Weight*. Lincoln, NE: iUniverse, 2007, p. 14.

24. Ana Cintado, "Eating Disorders and Gymnastics," Vanderbilt University Psychology Department. healthpsych.psy.vanderbilt.edu/HealthPsych/gymnasts.htm.

25. "USC Volleyball Star Talks Eating Disorders and Mental Health in Female Athletes," YouTube video, 3:57, posted by POPSUGAR, March 27, 2018. www.youtube.com/watch?v=Qqdbzqpc3QM.

26. “USC Volleyball Star Talks Eating Disorders and Mental Heath in Female Athletes,” YouTube video, posted by POPSUGAR.

27. Quoted in Lee Daniel Kravetz, “The Strange, Contagious History of Bulimia,” The Cut, July 31, 2017. www.thecut.com/article/how-bulimia-became-a-medical-diagnosis.html.

28. Kravetz, “The Strange, Contagious History of Bulimia.”

29. Quoted in Anna Duff, “Mel C Speaks About Battling an Eating Disorder While in the Spice Girls,” *Look*, October 4, 2017. www.look.co.uk/news/mel-c-eating-disorder-595972.

CHAPTER FOUR: HEALTH PROBLEMS

30. Quoted in Fred Bronson, *Billboard's Hottest Hot 100 Hits*, 3rd ed. New York, NY: Billboard Books, 2003, p. 48.

31. Quoted in Lindsey Getz, “Anorexia to Suicide—The Desperate Path,” *Social Work Today*, accessed on October 2, 2018. www.socialworktoday.com/news/enews_0812_01.shtml.

32. Quoted in Getz, “Anorexia to Suicide.”

CHAPTER FIVE: TREATING EATING DISORDERS

33. Steven Levenkron, *Anatomy of Anorexia*. New York, NY: W.W. Norton, 2000, p. 113.

34. Quoted in Kittleson, ed., *The Truth About Eating Disorders*, p. 136.

35. Quoted in Kittelson, ed., *The Truth About Eating Disorders*, p. 136.

36. Sacker, *Regaining Your Self*, p. 167.

37. Quoted in Aimee Liu, *Gaining*. New York, NY: Grand Central, 2008, p. 22.
38. Quoted in Liu, *Gaining*, p. 22.
39. Sacker, *Regaining Your Self*, pp. 129–130.
40. Quoted in Christina Chiu, *Eating Disorder Survivors Tell Their Stories*. New York, NY: Rosen, 1999, p. 50.
41. Quoted in Chiu, *Eating Disorder Survivors*, p. 51.
42. Quoted in Taylor, ed., *Going Hungry*, p. 297.
43. Quoted in Taylor, ed., *Going Hungry*, p. 301.
44. Quoted in Taylor, ed., *Going Hungry*, p. 301.

GLOSSARY

addiction: Physical, emotional, or psychological dependence on something.

anxiety: A mental illness characterized by irrational feelings of fear, worry, and unease.

body mass index (BMI): A calculation of weight relative to height.

calorie: A measure of energy intake and output.

criterion: A standard on which a judgment or decision may be based (plural: criteria).

depression: A mental illness characterized by feelings of hopelessness and sadness or numbness.

diabetes: A disease in which the body cannot control the amount of sugar in the blood because it does not have enough insulin.

diuretics: Chemicals used to increase urination and get rid of excess fluid.

hormone: A substance produced by the body that influences the way the body grows and develops.

hypothermia: A condition in which the temperature of the body gets very low.

hysteria: A state in which one's emotions get so strong they are uncontrollable.

laxative: A medicine that makes it easier for solid waste to pass through the body.

metabolism: The building-up and breaking-down processes of the body.

neurotransmitter: A substance that carries a signal from one nerve cell in the body to another.

nutrients: Substances that provide nourishment for the body.

proteins: Molecules made of amino acids that the body needs to function.

self-esteem: Self-respect; confidence in oneself.

serotonin: A chemical in the brain thought to be involved in depression and in the control of food intake.

theory: An idea that is intended to explain facts or events.

therapy: Treatment or counseling aimed at curing or managing physical or psychological problems.

ORGANIZATIONS TO CONTACT

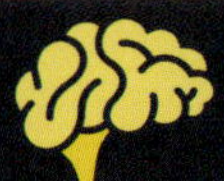

Eating Disorders Foundation of Canada
100 Collip Circle Research Park
Suite 230A
Western University
London, Ontario N6G 4X8
edfc.ca
Instagram: edf.canada
YouTube: EDFCTheHarbour
This nonprofit organization works to raise money for eating disorder research and advocacy.

The Emily Program
1295 Bandana Boulevard West
Suite 201
Saint Paul, MN 55108
emilyprogramfoundation.org
Instagram: emilyprogram
TikTok: emilyprogram
YouTube: EmilyProgram
This organization is dedicated to working to end eating disorders. Visitors to its website can take a quiz to see if they or a loved one is displaying disordered eating habits, contact a professional for help, and learn more about what treatment is like.

Families Empowered and Supporting Treatment of Eating Disorders (F.E.A.S.T.)
26F Congress Street
Suite 117
Saratoga Springs, NY 12866
feast-ed.org
Instagram: feast_ed
YouTube: FEAST-ED-Videos
F.E.A.S.T. works internationally to support those who take care of or love someone with an eating disorder. The organization gives information about these disorders and treatment. Additionally, it advocates for more research to help those with eating disorders.

National Association of Anorexia Nervosa and Associated Disorders (ANAD)
PO Box 409047
Chicago, IL 60640
helpline: (888) 375-7767
anad.org
Instagram: anadhelp
YouTube: ANADvideos
ANAD offers a phone helpline, operates a network of support groups for people with eating disorders and their families, and provides a list of health care professionals who treat eating disorders. It organizes national events and local programs and has a blog and YouTube channel full of information. All ANAD services are provided free of charge.

National Eating Disorders Association (NEDA)
333 Mamaroneck Avenue
Suite 214
White Plains, NY 10605
helpline: (800) 931-2237
nationaleatingdisorders.org
Instagram: neda
TikTok: neda
YouTube: NEDAonline
NEDA is the largest nonprofit organization in the United States working to prevent eating disorders and provide treatment information to those suffering from anorexia, bulimia, and binge eating disorders as well as those concerned with body image and related issues. NEDA also provides educational outreach programs and training for schools and universities.

FOR MORE INFORMATION 

BOOKS

Eason, Sarah, and Sarah Levete. *Having an Eating Disorder: Stories from Survivors.* Shropshire, UK: Cheriton Children's Books, 2022.

Gagne, Tammy. *What Are Eating Disorders?* San Diego, CA: BrightPoint Press, 2023.

Longe, Jacqueline L., and Grace Gallagher. *Empowering Teen Mental Fitness: A Guide for Managing Addiction, Eating Disorders, OCD, and Trauma.* Mason, OH: Gale, 2024.

Sharp, Katie John. *Pandemic Aftereffects: The Surge In Teen Eating Disorders.* San Diego, CA: ReferencePoint Press, 2023.

Sonenklar, Carol. *Not Just about Food: Understanding Eating Disorders.* Minneapolis, MN: Twenty-First Century Books, 2023.

WEBSITES

Eating Disorder Hope
eatingdisorderhope.com
Learn more about the ways those suffering from eating disorders can help themselves through recovery. Relatable and concrete tips, as well as links to other recovery articles, can encourage someone through the tough moments or inspire them to look for further help.

KidsHealth: Eating Disorders
kidshealth.org/en/teens/eat-disorder.html
This website gives more information about the symptoms and treatment for common eating disorders such as anorexia, bulimia, BED, and ARFID.

NEDA Resource Center
www.nationaleatingdisorders.org/resource-center
This area of the NEDA website helps people find eating disorder resources for themselves or a loved one.

YoungMinds: Body Image
www.youngminds.org.uk/young-person/coping-with-life/body-image
This website offers information about what body image is, advice on how to help yourself or a loved one cultivate a positive body image, and stories from teens who have struggled with mental health issues relating to their body.

INDEX

F

G

H

I

K

L

M

PHOTO CREDITS

Cover, p. 37 Pixel-Shot/Shutterstock.com; cover, pp. 1, 3-104 Trisno Wardana/Shuttestock.com; cover, p. 1, 3, 4, 6, 11, 25, 46, 61, 71, 87, 92, 94, 96, 98, 103, 104 Sentavio/ Shutterstock.com; p. 8 https://commons.wikimedia.org/ wiki/File:Karen_Carpenter_in_1972_White_House. png; p. 9 Joe Seer/Shutterstock.com; p. 12 https://en.m. wikipedia.org/wiki/File:Gull_-_Anorexia_Miss_A. jpg; p. 15 Pascal Huot/Shutterstock.com; pp. 17, 23, 48 New Africa/Shutterstock.coml; p. 21 Motortion Films/ Shutterstock.com; p. 24 Randy Miramontez/Shutterstock. com; p. 26 Yta23/Shutterstock.com; p. 28 Payless Images/ Shutterstock.com; p. 31 Monkey Business Images/ Shutterstock.com; pp. 43, 56 PeopleImages.com - Yuri A/ Shutterstock.com; p. 50 Minerva Studio/Shutterstock.com; p. 62 ridersuperone/Shutterstock.com; p. 65 marrishuanna/ Shutterstock.com; p. 69 Kathy Hutchins/Shutterstock.com; p. 74 SeventyFour/Shutterstock.com; p. 76 Gorodenkoff/ Shutterstock.com; p. 78 luchschenF/Shutterstock.com; p. 80 Pro.Sto/Shutterstock.com; p. 85 Prostock-studio/ Shutterstock.com.

ABOUT THE AUTHOR 

DONNA REYNOLDS is a freelance writer and editor who has worked on more than 50 books for young adults. She has a degree in English from the University of Wisconsin—Madison and spends as much time as possible traveling around the world. She tries to volunteer at a local nonprofit organization at least one day a week, no matter where she happens to be.